CLIMATE CHANGE AND CONFLICT PREVENTION

LESSONS FROM DARFUR

J. Andrew Plowman

National Intelligence University
Washington DC
September 2014

Dedication

To Wendy, Tessa, and Douglas, who keep me going.

In *Climate Change and Conflict Prevention: Lessons from Darfur*, J. Andrew Plowman uses the Darfur conflict as a case study to examine how the effects of climate change might lead to future violent conflicts, and assesses the best way to prevent these conflicts. In his research, Plowman reviews the environmental security literature and applies events from Darfur to climate change models. This research suggests that climate change is likely to increase the potential for intrastate and communal conflicts, as populations adjust to changes in the environmental systems that support their livelihoods. Ultimately, Plowman's examination of the Darfur conflict recommends a focus on structural conflict prevention through building adaptability to climate change and through the strengthening of institutions, particularly in fragile states.

The goal of the NI Press is to publish high-quality, valuable, and timely books on topics of concern to the Intelligence Community and the U.S. government. Books published by the NI Press undergo peer review by senior officials in the U.S. government and by outside experts.

How to order this book: Everyone may download a free electronic copy from our website at http://www.NI-U.edu. U.S. government employees may request a complimentary copy by contacting us at Press@ni-u.edu. The general public may purchase a copy from the Government Printing Office (GPO) at http://bookstore.gpo.gov.

Editor, NI Press
Office of Research
National Intelligence University
Defense Intelligence Agency
Joint Base Anacostia-Bolling
Washington, DC 20340-5100

Table of Contents

Chapter Four

Chapter Five

List of Figures

Acknowledgments

This study could not have become reality without the support of a large number of people. I would like to thank the staff at the Center for Strategic Intelligence Research (CSIR), who provided me with a warm place to hang my hat while I pursued this research. I am particularly grateful for comments, guidance, and encouragement from Solveig Brownfeld and Cathryn Thurston. Many others at CSIR served as informal sounding boards, including Bill Spracher, Jim Lightfoot, and fellow fellows Jason Stinchcomb, Greg Garland, Ed McClellan, and John Bitterman. Several others have given me useful comments and suggestions, including Jared Banks and Jennifer Bandy. Thanks to John Underriner for ensuring that I kept a suitably skeptical frame of mind.

Chapter One

Introduction, Methodology, and Literature Review

Introduction and Overview

There is a lively discussion in public policy circles and academia on the extent to which climate change can be expected to become a security problem. Several recent think tank reports and other studies classify catastrophic climate change as a great threat to U.S. and world security.[1] Kurt Campbell warns, for example, that "the United States must confront the harsh reality that unchecked climate change will come to represent perhaps the single greatest risk to our national security, even greater than terrorism, rogue states, the rise of China, or the proliferation of weapons of mass destruction." Separately, the CNA Corporation argues that climate change in the Middle East has the potential to exacerbate tensions over water: "The potential for escalating tensions, economic disruption, and armed conflict is great."[2] Others, such as Brown et al. or Dabelko, are more cautious, urging avoidance of hyperbole and warning against subsuming climate change into broader security challenges.[3]

Findings and statements such as those by Campbell and CNA, while not necessarily incorrect, are based on extreme scenarios for climate change. This study tries to answer the question of whether and how climate change would spark conflicts under a more likely "middle range" scenario for climate change (0.69 degrees Celsius increase in global mean temperatures by 2030 and 1.75 degrees Celsius by 2065, and sea level rises of 13 to 16 centimeters during the same period).[4] Such a midrange scenario is well within the expected range should current greenhouse gas emissions continue along expected trajectories. It is likely that the world will have to deal with the consequences of climate changes of this order of magnitude.

Research Question and Hypothesis

The purpose of this study is to explore the ways that the expected effects of intermediate-level climate change may affect human security and livelihoods, with a view to identifying risk factors for violent intrastate conflict and ways in which the international community might mitigate the potential for such conflict. It will seek to answer the question of how climate change might lead to violent conflict. Based on that exploration, the study will assess how such conflict might be prevented or mitigated and what role the international community can play in doing so.

The author's principal hypothesis at the outset is that climate change will increase the risk of violent intrastate conflicts, and that such conflicts will be a particular problem for fragile states. There are two alternate hypotheses: first, that climate change will not foster violent conflict; and, second, that if climate change does foster violent conflict, the international community is not well positioned to prevent such conflicts.

Chapter One—Introduction, Hypothesis, and Literature Review: This introductory chapter provides a brief review of the academic literature on environmental security.

Chapter Two—Expected Climate Changes: The study outlines expected climate changes under an intermediate climate change scenario, examines some of those climate changes on natural and human systems, and evaluates which populations are most vulnerable to climate changes.

Chapter Three—Darfur Case Study: The study will then turn to the concrete example of Darfur, where climate changes played a part in creating the conditions for violence. It will examine how the effects of climate changes thrust Darfur's nomadic groups into competition with settled farmers for water sources and land for grazing. Other political, economic, and social factors played a part in the tragic escalation of this conflict over time, and these will be reviewed in turn, with a view to identifying whether and how the conflict could have been prevented.

Chapter Four—Pathways Model and Vulnerability Screen: Chapter Four places the process that took place in Darfur into a broader model of the process through which climate changes might lead to conflicts, and examines what factors might be vulnerabilities. It also develops a vulnerability screen based on those factors, identifying several states that have a combination of physical and institutional vulnerabilities to climate change; these states are the most likely at risk of conflict resulting from climate change.

Chapter Five—Conflict Prevention and Recommendations: The final chapter analyzes the problem of preventing and mitigating climate change–related conflicts, and argues that the most effective ways to prevent climate change–related conflicts will be by increasing the adaptability of vulnerable populations and through institution building. It also makes several suggestions for those considering strategies to prevent and mitigate climate-related conflict risk. It will discuss the challenge posed by the goal of institutional strengthening, which is a key part of increasing adaptability to climate change, particularly where these local institutions may be corrupt, inhumane, and unrepresentative.

Summary of Research Results

There are always uncertainties when considering the future. Although case studies, including that of Darfur in Chapter Three, show there is a climate-conflict link in some cases, the existing cross-sectional quantitative research on environmental security does not clearly establish the size of the risk. Despite some uncertainties, this study finds that intermediate-scale climate changes are likely to increase the *potential* for intrastate and communal conflicts as populations adjust to changes in the environmental systems that support their livelihoods. This potential for conflict results when climate changes upset existing arrangements for the sharing of resources, such as water and agricultural land. This will occur in many cases either because of the direct effects of climate changes, such as droughts, flooding, sea-level rise, and long-term degradation of agricultural productivity, or indirect effects, such as the displacement of population groups, which can then upset previous balances in the migrant-receiving regions. Migrant flows such as these can transmit the effects of local or regional climate changes across international borders or even across continents.

Governing competition and disputes between competing users of resources is one of the fundamental functions of economic and sociopolitical systems. States with legitimacy across population groups, strong courts, developed institutional planning mechanisms, and strong economies are very likely to be able to manage these effects of climate change on the livelihoods of their people before they take on a dynamic with a potential for violence. The vulnerability screen developed in Chapter Four highlights several states that are particularly vulnerable to such dynamics.

Exploring under what conditions climate change may become a security problem is worthwhile for several reasons. First, climate change will exacerbate

Source: U.S. Geological Survey/Photo by Brent Hanson

the sort of climatic extremes that contributed to conflict in Darfur. Second, this study suggests that fragile states are particularly vulnerable to climate change–related conflicts; conflicts that can, in turn, reinforce economic and institutional failures. To the extent that states that are more fragile become failed states, they will pose a series of challenges to regional and international security. Third, prevention with diplomatic and development policy tools will invariably be cheaper, in both human and monetary terms, than dealing with disaster later.[5] Indeed, the last three U.S. national security policy documents articulated the position that conflict prevention is both cost-effective and improves security challenges posed by fragile and failing states.[6]

There is an important role for the international community to play in building adaptability to climate change. As explored in Chapter Five, two types of international community preventive interventions can help build adaptability to climate change and will also serve as structural conflict prevention measures. First are development projects that improve security of livelihoods, particularly through projects that improve access to water, agricultural yields, or both. Just as importantly, strengthening institutions in fragile states can pay dividends in terms of conflict prevention, as institutions will be key to increasing local adaptability to climate changes and mediating conflicts over water and land that are caused by such changes.

Institution building in fragile states, however, remains a process fraught with significant challenges and uncertainty. The international community has a poor record in this regard. More successful institution building will likely require revisiting some assumptions and priorities in development spending. Most importantly, it will require adopting a bottom-up approach to creating institution-building strategies that reflect the unique political, social, and economic situation in each country in an effort to build adaptability of these countries to climate change.

Literature Review: Previous Work on Environment and Conflicts

Despite a recent raft of think tank studies and mainstream media reports naming climate change as the next major security threat, the academic literature remains decidedly split on the relationship between climate and conflict.[7] Nevertheless, the potential for climate change–related conflicts has given new prominence to the literature on resource-scarcity and environmental conflicts. One prominent strand within this literature, known as neo-Malthusian, argues that when environmental degradation, population growth, and unequal distribution of resources combine, they create a situation of resource scarcity, which in turn can spark competition and conflict.[8] This argument contends that these conditions are already factors in conflicts and will be greater factors over time. The work of Homer-Dixon and that of Hauge and Ellingsen perhaps best exemplify this point of view.[9] Proponents see climate change as another factor that will exacerbate the problem of resource scarcity–related conflicts.[10]

Neo-Malthusian Argument: Scarcity Drives Conflict

A key part of the neo-Malthusian analysis of environmental scarcity–related conflicts is unequal access to renewable resources. Homer-Dixon in 1994 suggested two mutually reinforcing mechanisms, which he called "resource capture" and "ecological marginalization," through which environmental degradation and population pressure create conflicts over resource scarcity.

Resource capture is motivated, per Homer-Dixon, by a falling quality or quantity of renewable resources, which can lead a privileged group quickly to usurp ownership of the scarcer renewable resources at the expense of weaker groups. *Ecological marginalization* is a longer-term process in which inequalities in access to renewable resources, such as arable land, combine with population pressure to force migration into less productive areas. Homer-Dixon used incidents in the Philippines and Mauritania as examples of these processes.[11]

Environment Only One of Many Factors

A second strand of academic thinking criticized the work of the neo-Malthusians on both theoretical and methodological grounds, notably for underestimating the role played by political and economic institutions and for problematic statistical methodology. This strand has emphasized the importance of quantitative or empirical study of violent conflicts to produce findings that can be generalized. The works of Nils Gleditsch et al., Binningsbø et al., and Theisen, as well as works by Raleigh and Urdal, among others, have advanced this point of view.[12] Although this group acknowledges that certain cases suggest that resource scarcity can be a factor underlying the outbreak of organized violence, they note that there are always many other factors involved. This strand in the literature emphasizes that statistical studies show only a weak connection between resource scarcity and civil war.[13] One of these statistical studies, by Theisen, finds that "scarcity of natural resources has limited explanatory power in terms of civil violence, whereas poverty and dysfunctional institutions are robustly related to conflict."[14] Separately, an innovative approach by Raleigh and Urdal analyzes conflict data at the subnational level by using geospatial coordinate data on conflicts in Africa, and regresses those data against demographic variables, proxies for environmental scarcity, and economic and political variables. The results showed a moderately increased risk of violent conflicts because of water scarcity or degraded land, while the effects of political and economic variables on the outbreak of conflict in their quantitative model were much greater.[15] Such use of subnational data remains the exception rather than the rule in empirical studies, but could help in analysis of intrastate conflicts.

Three recent intriguing statistical studies looked at the association between rainfall *variability* and civil conflict. Miguel et al. focused on sub-Saharan

Africa, where reliance on rain-fed agriculture is high (only 1 percent of agricultural land is irrigated). This made rainfall variation a useful instrumental variable to correct for statistical limitations in other cross-sectional studies. The Miguel study posits that the transmission mechanism could be economic shock, as the fall in rainfall and, thereby, agricultural production changes personal calculation of opportunity costs for joining rebel groups. Miguel also cites case studies on Niger and Sierra Leone, where drought coincided with increased ability of rebel movements to recruit among less-than-fully-employed rural farmers or pastoralists, who had little motivation to remain on a farm and few other employment options.[16] In addition to Miguel, two other studies, one by Levy et al. and one by Hendrix and Glaser, found a significant effect of rainfall variation in one year on the likelihood of conflict in the next.[17] Levy et al. looked beyond Africa to global data for rainfall deviations and violent conflicts, with similar results.[18] The finding of each of these studies that rainfall variability affects conflict risk is important, particularly since climate change is expected to increase the variability of precipitation. Nevertheless, all three studies also found that institutional and economic variables had greater effects on conflict risk than rainfall variation.

Other quantitative studies have looked to history to serve as a guide for future climate-related conflicts. Zhang looked at Chinese history and found a significant correlation between *colder* weather and greater number of wars and instability in China over the last millennium.[19] Tol and Wagner took a similar approach, finding a significant correlation between colder weather and a greater number of wars in Europe in the second half of the previous millennium.[20] The results can be interpreted as supporting the idea that resource scarcity increases the likelihood of violent conflicts, as bad harvests during colder periods were highly correlated with an increased number of wars. Nunn examines the impact on Pacific rim and Pacific island societies of the comparatively fast shift in temperature and sea levels associated with the transition, from AD 1250 to AD 1350, from the relatively warm, wet "medieval temperature anomaly" to the "little ice age," a transition that apparently sparked strife and cultural retrenchment in many Pacific societies.[21] Like many others, these historical findings suggest a climate-conflict link operates under some circumstances, but does not settle important questions surrounding the chain of causality through which climate might influence conflict.

A Possible Approach to Understanding the Literature: Climate Change Exacerbates Other Variables

The apparently starkly contrasting views between the neo-Malthusians and those who doubt the explanatory power of environmental variables in conflicts were nicely bridged by Jared Diamond. Diamond argues, with regard to the Rwanda genocide, that environmental stress and demographic pressure will rarely be the proximate cause of violent conflict, but can be an important underlying factor. Environmental stress sets the stage, but the proximate causes will usually be political and economic factors that arise from the choices political leaders and societies make in response to those environmental stresses.[22] In a similar vein, Salehyan argues that "it is the interaction between environmental and political systems which is critical to understanding organized armed violence."[23]

Pathways from Environmental Stress to Economic and Political Conflict

To summarize, the quantitative studies of environmental change and conflict conducted to date show statistically significant, but weak, direct effects of environmental variables on violent intrastate conflict, and strong effects of institutional and economic variables on such conflict. The empirical work done so far, however, has not effectively modeled interactive effects between institutional variables and environmental pressures. The researchers could improve on their proxy data for governance and environmental stress. In addition, the reliance of most studies on country-level data when (in most cases) these conflicts are restricted to specific regions could affect the significance of their findings.[24] To the extent that institutions and political systems mediate the effects of environmental pressures, however, often with time lags and other factors playing a part, it is unlikely that the empirical studies as structured would show a strong direct effect of climate on conflict. The great majority of these studies looked at conflicts between government forces and armed opposition groups, not communal conflicts; but their findings suggest, and are consistent with, an indirect relationship between environmental pressures and an increased risk of violent intrastate conflict, especially in weakly governed states or regions.

But what is the real risk? The magnitude of risk that the current studies suggest is relatively low. The Hauge and Ellingsen study, for example, which showed the clearest support for the case that deforestation, land degradation, and low freshwater availability increase the risk of conflict, suggested that these raised the probability of civil war from a 1 percent base level to 1.5 percent, and of smaller communal conflicts from 4 percent to 8 percent.[25] The risk level results must be viewed with caution given the modeling and data limitations.

Impact of Climate Change on Human Security

The majority of the empirical studies in the environmental conflict literature tested for direct effects of environmental degradation on violent conflict. The presence or absence of violence, however, is only one aspect of security, which can be defined more broadly to include security of livelihoods and of the person. Barnett, drawing on an existing academic literature on human security, builds a prima facie case that the changes to earth's natural systems due to climate change threaten human security, broadly defined to include security of livelihoods.[26] The academic concept of human security is analogous to the "comprehensive concept of security" implemented by the Organization for Security and Cooperation in Europe (OSCE), which includes three aspects of security: (1) "traditional" security concerns involving armies and weapons; (2) economic and environmental aspects; and (3) human rights and governance aspects.[27] Viewed through this broader concept of human security, to the extent climate change reduces access to the natural resources (e.g., water, arable land) essential to livelihoods, it clearly becomes a security issue. In the context of the scenario that underlies this study, climate change will be a particular security problem for certain vulnerable populations. These findings are echoed by the work of the Intergovernmental Panel on Climate Change Fourth Assessment.[28]

Interstate War Less of an Issue

Notwithstanding the dramatic fall in the prevalence of interstate war since 1946, some authors have argued that water scarcity, including climate change–related water scarcity, will spark future wars between states. Joyce Starr's emblematic 1991 *Foreign Policy* article, "Water Wars," argues that growing competition over scarce water is likely to trigger violent international conflict, particularly in regions that lack much fresh water, such as the Middle East.[29] Others pick up this theme and argue that climate change will increase water scarcity and exacerbate existing conflicts between states, making them a flashpoint in the future.[30] A second camp, which includes work by Aaron Wolf et al., argues, based on empirical analysis of international conflict data, that water has never been a direct cause of conflict between states, but only a secondary source of tension. Yoffe et al., for example, empirically analyzed river basins and conflicts on global scale and found that countries generally cooperate over water, that water stress is not a significant source of conflict, and that drought does not increase the chance of conflict.[31] Wolf notes:

> Of course, people compete—sometimes violently—for water. Within a nation, users—farmers, hydroelectric dams, recreational users, environmentalists—are often at odds, and the probability of a mutually acceptable solution falls as the number of stakeholders rises. Water is never the single—and hardly ever the major—cause of conflict. But it can exacerbate existing tensions. History is littered with examples of violent water conflicts: just as Californian farmers bombed pipelines moving water from Owens Valley to Los Angeles in the early 1900s, Chinese farmers in Shandong clashed with police in 2000 to protest government plans to divert irrigation water to cities and industries. But these conflicts usually break out within nations.[32]

Like the environmental security literature, research on water conflicts suggests that many factors play a part. Gleditsch and collaborators in 2006 showed states with a higher level of development were less prone to water conflicts, suggesting that modernization, particularly the introduction of new water-efficient technologies and improved water management, can play a role in reducing such conflicts.[33] Gerlak and Grant's statistical analysis of cooperative agreements on trans-boundary waters highlights the growth of a web of treaties and international agreements to help govern trans-boundary rivers and lakes, but notes that there is still a considerable gap in the coverage of trans-boundary waters.[34] Nevertheless, as Yoffe et al. point out, once water-management treaties are signed, they prove remarkably durable; even states that have engaged in wars since 1946 (over other issues) have found it preferable to negotiate on the issue of water. Pakistan and India, and Israel and Jordan, stand out as positive examples.[35]

The Yoffe et al. finding is an important one, as there is a substantial network of treaties and international agreements to manage and defuse interstate water conflicts. These bilateral or regional agreements are supplemented with the information sharing, transparency enhancement, and conflict prevention played by international organizations, such as the United Nations and its specialized agencies, or regional organizations, such as the OSCE. This international governance framework makes interstate conflict over water less likely.

Initial Thoughts on Climate Change Literature

A few initial thoughts suggest themselves from this review of the academic literature:

(1) There is little evidence in the literature that the effects of climate change on the intermediate scale considered in this study would spark wars between states.

(2) Climate change is a danger particularly for the human security of vulnerable, less developed populations, especially in Africa.

(3) Several case studies of individual violent conflicts show a link between environmental factors and violent conflict, but their findings cannot be generalized.

(4) Broader quantitative studies of the links between environmental factors and violent intrastate conflict generally show a statistically significant, but weak, direct effect. Although several studies have replicated these results, data and modeling limitations mean that these findings do not constitute clear evidence for or against a climate-conflict link.

(5) The quantitative studies do show robust relationships between institutional and economic weakness and conflict risk. Since institutions and economies mediate the effects of environmental pressures, the empirical findings do not rule out the idea of an indirect pathway from environmental stress to conflict.

Studies of conflict outbreak that favor a particular factor as the key explanation for the onset of conflict are unconvincing. The complex and dynamic interaction of natural, social, and political-economic systems is very difficult realistically to replicate in models. At the same time, many studies contain a "kernel of truth" that can still be useful in considering vulnerability to climate change–related conflicts. In addition, the empirical analyses of violent conflict leave a series of questions unanswered, or only partially answered. Why, for instance, did drought and desertification play a role in the violent conflict in Darfur while many other poor and drought-stricken places, even in the same region, do not experience wide-scale violence? What risk factors might trigger environmental conflicts in other cases?

Data Sources

Data for the study will be drawn primarily from the relevant academic literature. Data for the vulnerability screen will be drawn from the World Bank Development Index and the Fragile States Index. Data on adaptation and institution building will be drawn from the development literature and from donor organizations such as the United Nations Development Program (UNDP), World Bank, and the Organization for Economic Cooperation and Development (OECD). The work of the Intergovernmental Panel on Climate Change (IPCC) will form a primary source for this study on the physical bases of climate change and many of its anticipated physical effects. Specifically, the IPCC's Fourth Assessment A1B scenario will serve as a baseline for considering the sociopolitical consequences of climate change. The A1B scenario is on the lower end of the intermediate scenarios assessed by the IPCC. It foresees atmospheric carbon dioxide levels stabilizing at concentration levels of about 650 parts per million. The scenario predicts an average of 0.69 degrees Celsius increase in global mean temperatures by 2030 and 1.75 degrees Celsius by 2065, and sea level rises of 13 to 16 centimeters. By the end of the century, temperatures would have risen, on average, 2.8 degrees Celsius (range from 1.7 to 4.4 degrees), and sea levels from 21 to 50 centimeters.[36]

Assumptions

This study assumes that the scientific consensus on climate change, as summarized in the reports of the United Nations' International Panel on Climate Change Assessment, is largely correct and that anthropogenic climate change is having, and will continue to have, substantial effects on the natural systems that support human life, with secondary effects on human societies and political systems. In light of the current politicization of debate over climate change, it is important to note that this study's findings on conflict risks will be relevant whatever the ultimate cause of climate change. This study also assumes that the United States will remain a global power over the course of the 21st century, with the capability and willingness to use its economic, diplomatic, political, and military power to influence events and decisions on a global scale.

Chapter Two

A Brief Survey of Climate Change, or What to Expect when You're Expecting Climate Change

This chapter briefly outlines expected climate changes and some of their direct effects on natural and human systems, to inform the exploration in later chapters of how these effects on natural systems and human systems may lead to violent conflict and of how best to mitigate the risk of such conflicts.

Climate Science Process

This study is not about climate science. Putting aside the current political debate that surrounds proposed measures to mitigate and adapt to climate change, the study assumes that the existing scientific consensus that human emissions of greenhouse gases are altering the earth's climate is correct. Regardless of the ultimate cause of climate change, many of the findings of this study on how these changes may lead to violent conflict are still applicable.

It is instructive to highlight a few indicators of the strength of the consensus among climatologists and scientists who work in related fields. A 2004 survey of 928 papers published in peer-reviewed scientific journals concerning global climate change found that none of these

> *"One of the brightest gems in the...weather is the dazzling uncertainty of it."*
>
> —Mark Twain

articles opposed the view that anthropogenic, or human-caused, climate change is occurring; 75 percent explicitly endorsed that conclusion while 25 percent concerned research of past climate (paleoclimate) and took no specific position on anthropogenic climate change today.[37] This is not to imply that there is no uncertainty or that the current understanding is perfect. As with other realms of scientific inquiry, new findings are published constantly, illuminating what previously were poorly understood aspects of the earth's systems or challenging previous assumptions. But the basic mechanics of the process of climate change are well enough understood and widely enough accepted that on October 21, 2009, the heads of 18 American scientific associations, including the American Meteorological Society, the American Geophysical Union, the American Association for the Advancement of Science, and the American Chemical Society, sent a joint letter to the U.S. Congress reiterating that there is scientific consensus that climate change is occurring, that human emission of greenhouse gases is a "primary driver" of these changes, and that climate change would have broad impacts on society and environmental systems. The letter urged that emissions of greenhouse gases be reduced "dramatically" in order to avoid the most severe consequences of climate change.[38] The heads of nine national academies of sciences, including China, Brazil, Russia, the United States, and the remaining member countries of the Group of Eight (G-8) industrialized countries have made a similar statement, calling for a "global response" to climate change.[39]

The most comprehensive summarization of the state of scientific understanding of the phenomenon of climate change is the Fourth Assessment Report (AR4), published in 2007 by the United Nations Intergovernmental Panel on Climate Change (IPCC). The IPCC was formed under the auspices of the World Meteorological Organization and the United Nations Environmental Program specifically to "assess on a comprehensive, objective, open and transparent basis the scientific, technical, and socioeconomic information relevant to understanding the scientific basis of risk of human-induced climate change, its potential impacts and options for adaptation and mitigation." The IPCC supports the UN Framework Convention on Climate Change, the goal of which is to avoid dangerous human interference with the earth's climate. Their reports are based on peer-reviewed scientific publications and are themselves reviewed both by other experts and by representatives of the governments that are members of the panel.[40]

The work of the IPCC will form the primary source for this study on the anticipated effects of climate change. Specifically, the IPCC's Fourth Assessment A1B scenario will serve as a baseline for considering the sociopolitical consequences of climate change. The A1B scenario is on the lower end of the intermediate warming scenarios assessed by the IPCC. It foresees atmospheric carbon dioxide levels stabilizing at concentration levels of about 750 parts per million, up from the December 2009 level of 387.3 parts per million. The scenario predicts an average of 0.69 degrees Celsius increase in global mean temperatures by 2030 and 1.75 degrees Celsius by 2065, and sea level rises

Figure 1: The IPCC A1B Scenario

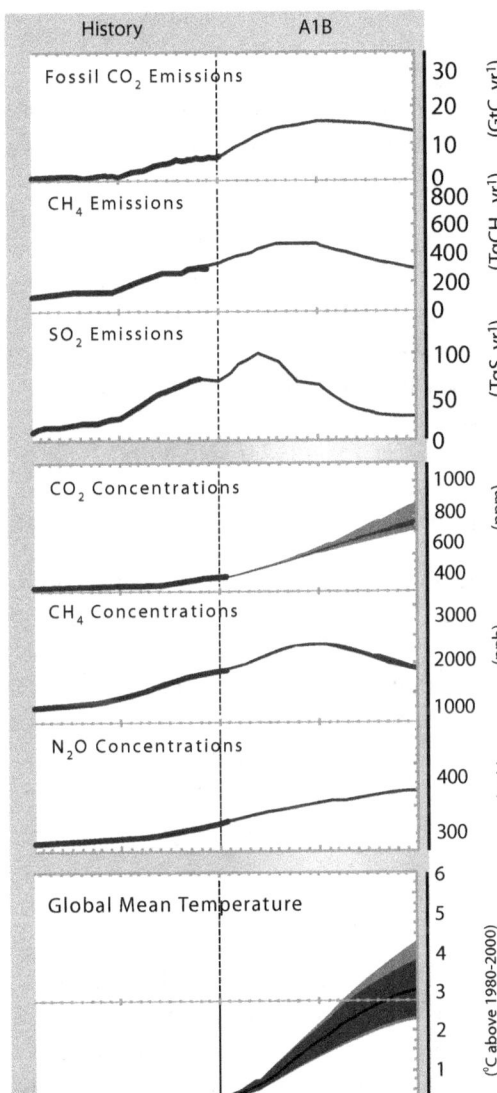

Source: Climate Change 2007: The Physical Science Basis. Working Group I Contribution to the Fourth Assessment Report of the Intergovernmental Panel on Climate Change, Figure 10.26 (left column). Cambridge University Press.

of 13 to 16 centimeters. By the end of the century, temperatures would have risen, on average, 2.8 degrees Celsius (range from 1.7 to 4.4 degrees) and sea levels risen from 21 to 50 centimeters.[41]

Although the A1B scenario foresees reductions in greenhouse gas emissions, it is not predicated on successful negotiation of a particular emissions target. This mid-range scenario foresees the widespread adoption of resource-efficient technologies and reductions in the material intensity of economies (i.e., the amount of energy and basic material inputs, such as metals used to generate each unit of economic output, would fall). Therefore, living standards among countries would continue to converge at a high level. The scenario foresees global population peaking at about 9 billion by the middle of the 21st century and declining slightly thereafter. It posits an emphasis on global solutions to economic and environmental sustainability, but no additional climate initiatives beyond agreement on a successor to the 1997 Kyoto Protocol of the United Nations Framework Convention on Climate Change (UNFCCC), the first agreement to call for limiting greenhouse gas emissions.[42]

Negotiations to fashion a workable successor arrangement to the Kyoto Protocol and to reduce future emissions of greenhouse gases are ongoing as of this writing. Regardless of whether they occur as part of a comprehensive global agreement, reductions in greenhouse gas emissions will help limit the severity of future climate change. Some greenhouse gases, notably carbon dioxide, linger in the atmosphere for decades. Since today's carbon dioxide emissions will contribute to warming the global climate for at least the next 40 to 50 years, it is important to evaluate their potential impacts on natural systems and human institutions.[43]

Definitions: Weather, Climate, and Variability

Mark Twain is said to have commented once that "climate is what you expect; weather is what you get." Building a little onto Twain's definitions, weather includes the meteorological conditions at a given point in time, including temperature, humidity, air pressure, and precipitation. Climate is probably most easily defined as average weather over an extended period of time.[44] Both weather modeling and climate modeling are enormously complex undertakings. The most sophisticated computerized weather prediction models available today are inaccurate beyond five or six days because weather systems are highly

Figure 2: Expected Changes in Mean Temperature

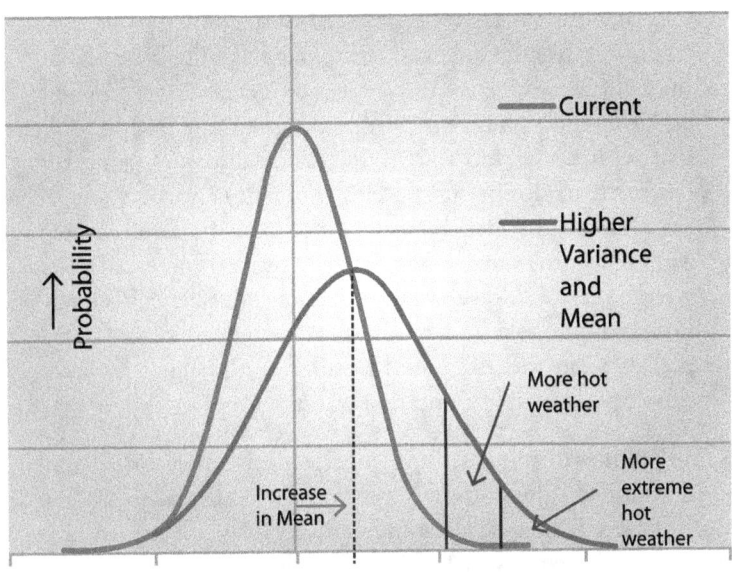

Source: Adapted from the IPCC Third Assessment Report

sensitive to small changes in conditions, so even small errors in forecasting compound quickly. Despite the challenges of predicting the weather, understanding climate as average weather over a certain time period allows us to consider changes in climate in terms of a statistical distribution of weather events around a mean (average) value, as depicted graphically in Figure 2.[45] This figure illustrates the finding, which the IPCC Fourth Assessment states is 90 percent to 99 percent probable, of both increased average temperatures and variability in temperatures.[46] Variability is more difficult to prepare for than a more consistent climate because the number of extreme weather events, including heat waves, storms, floods, etc., is expected to increase.

Disruption of Precipitation Patterns

Most climate models agree that global average rainfall will increase with climate change, as the additional heat intensifies the hydrological cycle of evaporation, cloud formation, and precipitation.[47] That average, however, conceals dangerous increases in extreme events of both flooding and drought.

An IPCC technical paper states:

> Globally, the negative impacts of future climate change on freshwater systems are expected to outweigh the benefits. By the 2050s, the area of land subject to increasing water stress due to climate change is projected to be more than double that with decreasing water stress. Areas in which runoff is projected to decline face a clear reduction in the value of the services provided by water resources. Increased annual runoff in some areas is projected to lead to increased total water supply. However, in many regions, this benefit is likely to be counterbalanced by the negative effects of increased precipitation variability and seasonal runoff shifts in water supply, water quality, and flood risks.[48]

The IPCC predicts the intensity of precipitation events will vary by three standard deviations from current levels over the course of the 40- to 50-year scenarios they studied, while the number of dry days will vary by 0.5 standard deviations from current levels.[49] For Africa, the IPCC predicts:

> Warming is very likely (greater than 90% probability) to be larger than the global annual mean warming throughout the continent and in all seasons, with drier subtropical regions warming more than the moister tropics. Annual rainfall is likely (greater than 66% probability) to decrease in much of Mediterranean Africa and the northern Sahara, with a greater likelihood of decreasing rainfall as the Mediterranean coast is approached. Rainfall in southern Africa is likely to decrease in much of the winter rainfall region and western margins. There is likely to be an increase in annual mean rainfall in East Africa. It is unclear how rainfall in the Sahel, the Guinean Coast and the southern Sahara will evolve.[50]

The World Bank expects water scarcity to be a greater problem than it is today:

> Water is the major vulnerability in the Middle East and North Africa, the world's driest region, where per capita water

availability is predicted to halve by 2050 even without the effects of climate change. The region has few attractive options for increasing water storage, since close to 90 percent of its fresh¬water resources are already stored in reservoirs.[51]

Impact on Agriculture: Declining Calorie Availability in Developing Countries

Climate change will harm agricultural production in several ways, including through the effects of increased temperatures on plant life and by increasing the variability of precipitation. Higher variability and more extreme weather events are expected to lead to increased incidence of flooding, which will have secondary effects on soil fertility as nutrient-rich topsoil is eroded and washed off previously fertile fields. The International Food Policy Research Institute (IFPRI), which has received funding from the U.S. government, among other donors, explains how climate change can be expected to affect agricultural production:

> Agriculture is extremely vulnerable to climate change. Higher temperatures eventually reduce yields of desirable crops while encouraging weed and pest proliferation. Changes in precipitation patterns increase the likelihood of short-run crop failures and long-run production declines. Although there will be gains in some crops in some regions of the world, the overall impacts of climate change on agriculture are expected to be negative, threatening global food security.[52]

Declining Calorie Intake: There have been several attempts to put hard numbers on some of these phenomena. The International Food Policy Research Institute estimates are based on coupling climate models to agricultural production models to forecast some of the potential effects of climate change on agricultural production. Absent significant investments to increase yields—a point to be expanded on later—the institute predicts a drop of almost 10 percent in calorie availability (over 200 calories) in developing countries by 2050, from the year 2000 value of 2,696 kilo-calories per capita. South Asia and sub-Saharan Africa would be particularly hard hit. Child malnutrition, which can have lifelong effects on the individual's health and potential productivity, also would increase by an estimated 20 percent relative to the no-climate-change scenario.[53] The agricultural sectors in many developing countries remain highly vulnerable to increased rainfall variations.[54] In the words of a farmer from Mozambique, "Hunger is the lack of rain."[55]

Higher Food Prices: Falls in agricultural yields combined with an increase in the world's population (to a predicted plateau of 9.1 billion by 2050) should also increase food prices beyond what these grains would cost in a no-climate-change scenario.[56] The IFPRI calculated price increases from 32 percent to 111 percent for staples such as wheat, rice, and corn by the year 2050; soybeans fared better at only 10–14 percent higher.[57]

Loss of Livelihoods: The undermining of agricultural productivity could have problematic secondary effects on development in many countries, as agriculture is a key sector for development efforts. Taxes on agricultural surpluses helped finance the industrial revolution in the 19th century. While today, agriculture is the source of only 2 percent of GDP in developed countries, it accounts for 11 percent of GDP in developing countries, and 40 percent in Africa.[58] Its importance for many developing countries is difficult to overstate:

> Globally, it is the source of livelihood for about 85 percent of the rural people, and in Africa, where more than 80% of the population is rural, subsistence agriculture accounts for the livelihoods of about 90% of the these rural people, most of them living below official poverty lines.[59]

Famine: Some historians have begun looking for historical parallels of climate variability. What may have been the most devastating famines in history occurred in India and China from 1876 to 1879, where the failure of the annual monsoon rains for three consecutive years, associated with a particularly intense El Niño–Southern Oscillation (ENSO) event, was complicit in the deaths of six to ten million persons in British India and ten to twenty million persons in China.[60] A complicating factor in that famine may have been the emergence around that time of a wave of globalization powered by the steam engine and the telegraph, which created an early version of a global market for grain. The droughts created a supply shock and drove prices well above the ability of many to buy food to replace their lost household food production.[61] The availability of better relief and food aid mechanisms, combined with modern transportation, would likely make it harder for future droughts to cause mortality on such a scale. But global markets and skyrocketing prices for food in such a situation would still be a burden for the poor, globally.

Health and Disease

Like some historians, biologists and epidemiologists have begun using ENSO as a proxy for climate change to examine how climate change may cause variations in disease patterns over time. Based on such studies, as well as on other work, they expect that climate change will affect human health both directly and indirectly.[62]

Heat Waves and Flooding: The direct effects of climate change include extreme weather events, notably heat waves and flooding. There is clear evidence that heat waves are associated with increases in mortality in the short term. The incidence of flooding is expected to increase as precipitation becomes more variable and the hydrological cycle intensifies. Increased flooding will have direct effects on mortality through drowning, and secondary effects if the floods damage sanitation and health infrastructure.[63]

Infectious Disease: Among the predicted indirect effects of climate change will be an increased prevalence of certain infectious diseases, particularly those which are hosted or transmitted by vectors (like mosquitoes) that will find a warmer and, on average, wetter world a more favorable habitat in which to live and breed. For example, more of the world's surface will be hospitable to the vectors that transmit tropical diseases and parasitic infections, notably malaria, dengue fever, and leishmaniasis.[64]

Loss of Productivity Due to Sickness: Although increased prevalence of disease is a concern in and of itself, disease also has been shown to contribute to the cycle of poverty as the productivity and earnings of the sick decline.[65] In cases of epidemics and pandemics, such as the HIV pandemic, the economic growth of entire countries may be affected.[66] To the extent that climate change increases the prevalence of infectious diseases, it will increase the challenge of addressing poverty and economic development in some countries. Effective adaptation strategies can help mitigate some of these disease

Figure 3: Expected Change in Agricultural Productivity by 2050 under Current Practices

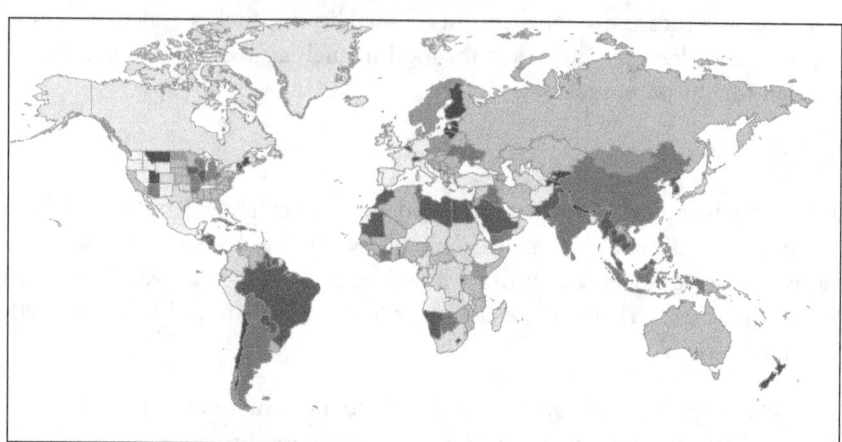

Used with Permission. Source: World Bank and Müller et al., 2009, "Climate Change Impacts on Agricultural Yields." *Note:* The coloring in the figure shows the projected percentage change in yields of 11 major crops from 2046 to 2055, compared with 1996–2005.

risks, but making these investments will strain the resources of many developing nations.

Sea Level Rise

The increase in sea levels expected under the scenario that forms the baseline for this study is not extreme: 13 to 16 centimeters by 2065 and 21 to 50 centimeters by the end of the century.[67]

Migration: These increases are nevertheless sufficient to pose a significant problem for certain vulnerable populations and low-lying agricultural land, which will be exposed to salt-water intrusion, erosion, and submersion, notably in the populous Nile delta, in the Mekong River delta in Vietnam and Cambodia, and in Bangladesh.[68] The predicted increase in storm surges noted above will exacerbate this problem. The affected population of such low-lying areas world-wide is an estimated 56 million.[69] How the affected communities will adapt is not well established, although some studies speculate that these effects will spark large-scale migration from the affected low-lying areas.[70]

Figure 4 summarizes the expected climate changes, their direct and indirect impacts on environmental systems, and who is most vulnerable to each of these changes.

Figure 4: Expected Climate Changes and Impacts			
Climate Change	Direct Impact	Secondary Impact	Most Vulnerable
• Increased average temperatures • Increased variability of temperature and precipitation • Increase in extreme weather events • Thermal expansion of oceans and melting of glaciers	• Widespread disruption in precipitation patterns • Droughts in some places, increased flooding in others	• Falling agricultural yields • Increase in regions subject to water stress	• Regions dependent on rain-fed agriculture • Rural poor in developing countries
	• Extension of favorable habitat for certain disease vectors	• Increased prevalence of tropical diseases	• Rural and urban poor in developing countries
	• Sea level Rise	• Flooding of low-lying coastal areas • Erosion of agricultural land • Salt water intrusion into aquifers	• Heavily populated coastal agricultural regions such as the Nile Delta, the Mekong River delta, and the Ganges/Brahmaputra River delta • Small island states

Sources: IPCC, Bonds et al. (2009), World Health Organization, International Food Policy Research Institute, World Bank, Dasgupta et al. (2007).

Chapter Three

Darfur: Drought, Disruption, and War

Overview of Darfur's Geography, History, and Identity

Most contemporary accounts of the conflict in Darfur begin with the outbreak of conflict in 2003, when two armed Darfurian rebel movements began attacks on government targets. The bloody conflict—which has led to roughly 300,000 dead and 2.7 million displaced—included pervasive instances of mass killings and ethnic cleansing that the U. S. government described as a case of genocide directed against the Fur people.[71] In addition to the human tragedy of these events, political reverberations are still being felt: in 2009, the International Criminal Court indicted Sudanese President Umar al-Bashir for war crimes and crimes against humanity, yet he remains in power.[72]

The roots of the Darfur conflict, however, run much deeper into the past. Indeed, the emergence of organized, armed Darfurian opposition groups in 2003 was preceded by two decades of conflict in which periods of heavy fighting were interspersed with failed peace agreements and lower levels of fighting, all of which led to the atrocities of 2003.

This case study analyzes the roots of the Darfur conflict. Events and data that touch on three themes will be highlighted as the story of the conflict unfolds. The first theme involves failures of governance. The second theme relates to the climatic changes that occurred in the Sahel, of which Darfur forms a part, and their effects on the livelihoods of its inhabitants. The third theme encompasses conflict group formation, a process in which radical ideology played a part.

This study argues that those three forces—climate changes, failed governance, and conflict group formation—combined to harden latent ethnic divisions and to cause the outbreak of serious organized violence in the 1987–1989 Arab Fur war, an event that witnessed the initial emergence of the infamous Janjawiid tribal militia, a full decade and a half before the conflict gained international exposure in 2003.

This chapter will set the stage for an examination of events in these three thematic forces with a brief overview of Darfur's history, geography, and identity.

Geographically, Darfur forms part of the Sahel, a semi-arid belt south of the Sahara Desert, ranging from the very arid north on the edge of the desert to the forest savannah of the south.[73] The central portion of Darfur contains the Jebel Marra highlands, which contain the richest soil and receive the highest rainfall in Darfur.[74] Darfur is about the size of France, and its population is between 6 and 7 million. Unlike most of the rest of Sudan, which lies in the Nile basin, most of Darfur forms part of the Lake Chad watershed.[75]

Darfur, which means "land of the Fur," is located in what is today western Sudan. Between 1630 and 1917, Darfur formed the core of an independent sultanate, the Keira Sultanate, which was centered on the Jebel Marra highlands. These highlands are the cultural and historic heartland of Darfur.[76] The Keira dynasty, founded around 1630 by Sulayman Solong, was ethnically Fur, but Solong transformed what had been an ethnically based tribal kingdom into a multi-ethnic sultanate, governing a mixed population. O'Fahey notes that the sultans ruled through a "title-holding elite recruited from all major ethnic groups."[77]

Today, the Fur make up about a third of Darfur's population, and have been an ethnic minority within broader Darfur since the beginning of the sultanate.[78] The Keira Sultanate existed for almost three centuries, from about 1630 until British conquest in 1916, with one interregnum from 1874 to 1898, a period when Darfur was initially taken over by the Ottomans and then ruled by the Mahdist rebels.[79] Islam spread peacefully to Darfur, brought by itinerant Sufi mystics; the sultans embraced Islam and the Arabic language as agents of modernization. According to Flint and de Waal:

> By 1800, the Fur sultanate was the most powerful state within the borders of modern-day Sudan. In adopting Islam as the official state religion, the Fur sultans also embraced Arabic as a language of religious faith, scholarship, and jurisprudence. Both Arabic and Fur were spoken at court. Darfurians—like most Africans—were comfortable with multiple identities. Dar Fur was an African kingdom that embraced Arabs...[80]

The economy of the Keira Sultanate in Darfur was based on traditional agriculture, with nomadic and semi-nomadic herding of cattle, camels, sheep,

Figure 5: Map of Sudan

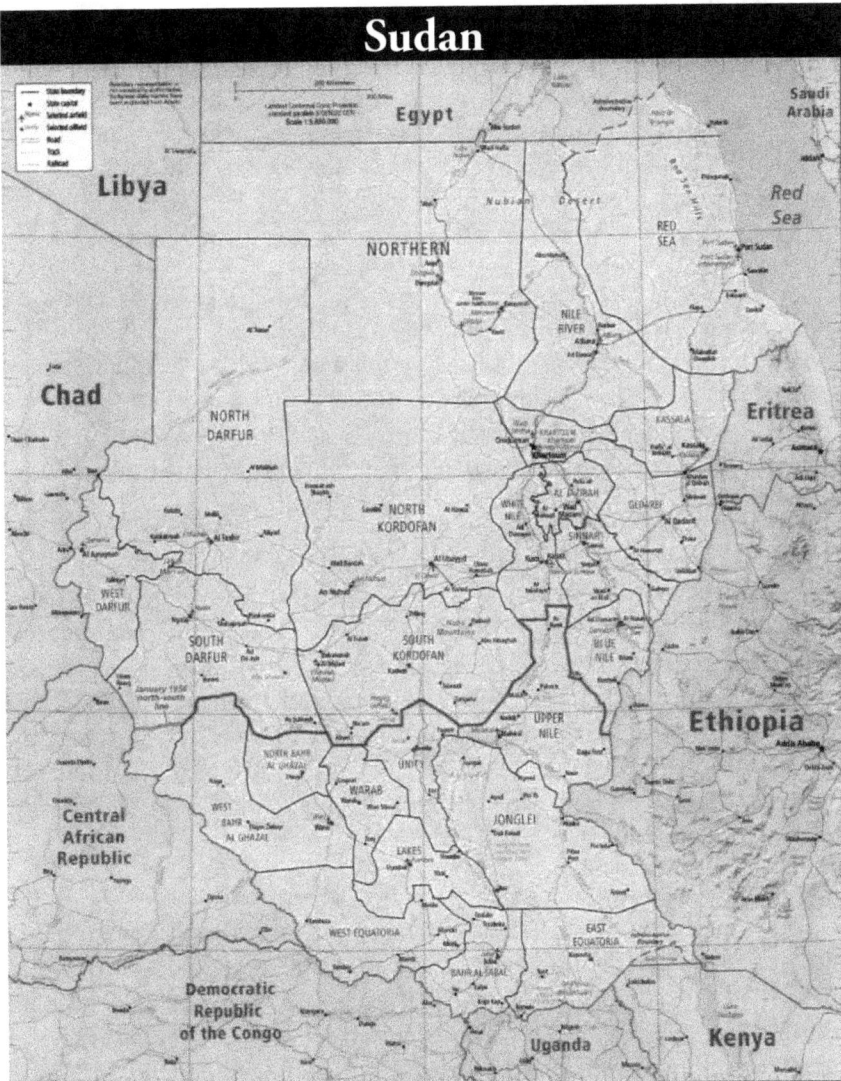

Source: CIA; https://www.cia.gov/library/publications/cia-maps-publications/
maps/777526.jpg

and goats. Trade, including the slave trade, brought much-needed revenue for the sultanate. Bassil notes that:

> Extensive trade relations with the west and the north also added to the ethnic diversity of Dar Fur as traders from north and northeast sought goods supplied by Dar Fur and obtained in the regions from the southern boundaries of the Sultanate, especially slaves, but also items such as ostrich feathers and ivory which the Keira acquired by raiding into central Africa.[81]

Although the sultanate did engage in raiding and conquest, including its 1787 conquest of the neighboring Kordofan Sultanate, Bassil notes that peaceful methods of expansion, including intermarriage with and co-option of rival groups, were important in Darfur's history. Such tactics would have been preferred as the Fur were never a majority group in the sultanate.[82]

The relative remoteness of Darfur may have been a factor in its survival into the 20th century as an independent entity. According to Bassil, who draws on the works of Warburg and Theobald, when the Anglo-Egyptian condominium took over the Nile provinces of Sudan, it was reluctant to extend its rule to the outlying province of Darfur. Cromer, the British consul-general to Egypt, vetoed a plan to conquer the region and annex it, stating that undertaking the direct government of Darfur would be a useless and expensive burden. So, while Ali Dinar, the last sultan, was informed that his sultanate lay within an Anglo-Egyptian sphere of influence, the British allowed him wide latitude in dealing with local affairs.[83]

There is disagreement among scholars as to the precise reasons the British changed their minds in 1916 and took over Darfur. Bassil states that the decision was primarily due to the fear that the French, who had colonized what is now Chad, would take over Darfur as well.[84] Daly blames machinations by the British commander in Khartoum, General Wingate, who used provocations and allegations of Ottoman collusion with Ali Dinar to justify an invasion.[85] Collins alludes to the possible role Islam may have played in Ali Dinar's decision to support the Turks, as fellow Muslims.[86] In addition to hostility toward the allies, Robinson notes Ali Dinar's refusal to honor a previous pledge to pay tribute to the British as a factor in his downfall.

Moreover, Ali Dinar had been fighting the French on his western border, and may have regarded the French-British wartime alliance as a betrayal by the British.[87] Regardless of the precise reasons, Ali Dinar and his sons fled the Darfurian capital of El Fasher after the defeat of their army in 1916, and were subsequently hunted down and killed. Darfur was absorbed into the British Empire in January 1917, with a few western provinces of the sultanate, including Dar Tama, Dar Sila, and Dar Qimr, given to French colonial governance.[88]

Britain had little interest in its new conquest. Flint and de Waal note that:

> Britain's only interest in Darfur was keeping order. It administered the province with absolute economy. The core of this was the "Native Administration" system, by which chiefs administered their tribes on behalf of the government ... tolerating the idiosyncrasies of local potentates provided that their abuses were not too egregious and they kept the peace.[89]

The native administration system's elimination by the Sudanese government decades later would play an unfortunate role in the outbreak of violence in the latter portions of the 20th century.[90]

Two observations on Darfur's history are relevant to the exploration of the origins of the conflict in the last two decades of the 20th century. First, as de Waal points out, the process of state formation in Darfur was separate from that which occurred in the Nile region or in southern Sudan. Second, ethnic identity per se was not a significant source of violent conflict.[91]

Ecological Zones and Eking Out a Living in Darfur

To understand why the environmental crisis that resulted from climate changes beginning in the 1970s had the ultimate impacts it did, one must start with an understanding of Darfur's three ecological zones. These zones are inhabited by different groups whose traditional ways of life were adapted to the climatic niches they occupied. The northern zone lies on the edge of the Sahara, is arid, and has been inhabited primarily by nomadic groups, who are predominantly camel herders. Of these, most are Juhayna Arab Bedouins.[92]

The majority of Darfur's Arab groups arrived in Darfur between the 14th and 18th centuries. The largest group were Juhayna Bedouins who arrived from the west, while small numbers of scholars and merchants arrived from the east and west. The Juhayna Bedouins split into two groups that retained their nomadic lifestyles: the Baggara (literally, "cattle people") who moved mainly to the south, and Abbala (literally, "camel herders") to the north.[93] The latter northern Abbala group includes a section known as the Northern Rizeigat, the ruling family of which included the Janjawiid leader Musa Halil.[94] Other northern groups include the non-Arab Zaghawa and the Arab Zayyadiya. The nomadic groups migrate seasonally as far as 300 miles, twice a year, and further in dry years.[95]

The central part of Darfur, including the Jebel Marra highlands, was the traditional heart of the Fur Sultanate, but also home to several other non-Arab groups. The Fur and other groups here, including the Masalit, Gama, Tama, Qimr, Tunjur, Mima, and others, practice settled agriculture. While the highlands, with their volcanic soils, have been the most propitious area of Darfur for farming, they too have been affected by drought and soil degradation, though not to the degree affecting Darfur's northern belt. Farmers in Darfur move around as well, particularly in dry eastern Darfur where "villages grow and die along with their water supplies and the fertility of their soils."[96]

Southern Darfur has more rainfall than the north, but is less suitable for farming than Jebel Marra. It serves as the main corridor for Baggara (cattle-herding) migration; different Baggara groups herd livestock between Lake Chad and the Nile River. Several different groups of Baggara Arabs live here, including the Beni Halba, Habbaniyya, Taisha, and Rizeigat clans, the last being the most powerful.[97] Each of these Baggara groups in the south was given a large land grant (hakura) by the Fur sultans, while the northern Abbala cousins were not.[98]

The many different tribal and ethnic groups of Darfur managed to work out a mostly peaceful coexistence. The Fur and the Baggara, according to Barth, were economically symbiotic. Fur farmers who were doing well would invest in cattle and entrust them to the Baggara or, in some cases, begin migrating with the Baggara and adopt an "Arab" lifestyle.[99] In the north, sedentary groups had a tradition, later interrupted, of entrusting their camels to the Arab Abbala camel herders. Camels were important to long-distance trade, and such arrangements were mutually beneficial.[100] Traditional life in Darfur, while hardscrabble and often desperate, had a pattern in which different groups took advantage of niches and complementary activities:

> Traditionally, the nomads spent the rains (June-Sept) and the following three months, October to December, in the desert, grazing their camels on the succulent pastures along Wadi Howar, the last seasonal watercourse before the desert, and further north, where the grasses known as Jizu are so succulent that camels can go without water for more than thirty days. Until just a few years ago, this rich grazing land was shared among Darfur's camelmen: Arabs, Zaghawa, and Meidob. In January, the herds move south, spending the winter and dry season in the valleys south of Kutum or traveling into the well-watered districts of south-west Darfur, along three major migration routes that everyone shares.[101]

Ethnicity and Identity

Identity and ethnicity are a complex subplot in the Darfur conflict. Historically, ethnicity and identity in Darfur were, for most groups, linked to the environmental and climatic niches they occupied and the livelihoods they pursued. Per Flint and de Waal, "A host of ethnic groups or tribes—between forty and ninety, depending on one's definition—have emerged from Darfur's history."[102] Despite the current polarization and conflict, intermarriage between different groups was common and sometimes used to consolidate alliances among tribal groups. The leading families all have mixed parentage.[103] The "polyglot" Keira Sultanate integrated diverse groups. Bassil argues that its history was "not dominated by issues of ethnicity or tribalism."[104] In a similar vein, de Waal argues that

> [f]rom the viewpoint of Southern Sudan, "African" and "Arab" are polar opposites. From the viewpoint of Darfur (late in the Sultanate), the distinction between "Arab" and "African" did not arise. Darfurians had no difficulty with multiple identities, and indeed would have defined their multi-ethnic kingdom as encompassing Arabs, both Bedouins and cultural Arabs.[105]

After 1917, the various tribes of Darfur, despite their unique history and life-styles, began a process of assimilation into the dominant (i.e., Nile-based) Sudanese society and politics. Many traditions among the Arab Bedouin tribes and the non-Arab groups began to be discarded.[106] Use of the jellabiya and taub clothing, shunning of alcohol, and a less independent role for women became the norm. The process of assimilation into Sudanese society and politics was advanced, according to Doornbos, by teachers, traders, fundamentalist preachers, and officials from the dominant Jellaba Arab society who came to Darfur from the Nile regions of Sudan.[107] This overall process of assimilation continued despite brief flirtations by some Darfurians with clandestine independence movements in the early 1960s.[108]

For a period of time, identities were fluid, influenced both by the dominant Sudanese Nile-based culture and by Darfur's history of ethnic mingling. Flint and de Waal note the example of one village, Dor, as follows:

> Twenty-five years ago, the village (Dor) was dominated by four ethnic groups: Zaghawa, Fur, Tunjur, and Kaitinga. But some would argue that Fur and Tunjur are parts of the same ancient group, and that Kaitinga straddles all three. Plus two categories of Arabs: Jellaba and Rizeigat. The Jellaba are traders from the Nile. The Rizeigat are local Darfur Bedouins, members of the Mahamid section, Aald Tako clan…. But that didn't stop almost half the marriages in Dor crossing ethnic lines.[109]

For a time, Darfurians were comfortable with multiple identities, all of which had different economic roles, but failures of governance, climate change, and conflict group formation led to a hardening of identity along ethnic lines.

Failures of Governance

Failure of governance, particularly of conflict prevention mechanisms, played a key part in allowing the escalation of the Darfur conflict. When Britain conquered Darfur, it was for reasons external to Darfur, so Britain's primary interest in Darfur became simply to keep the peace so it could focus its resources elsewhere.[110] To do so, Britain implemented a system it labeled "Native Administration," or indirect rule, in which tribal leaders continued governing their people and regions; indeed, their role in some cases was strengthened by the judicial power given them to mediate disputes.[111] The British also set about regularizing land grants (known as *dar* and *hakura*) given under the sultanate; in so doing, they sought primarily to codify existing land use arrangements, but not to alter them significantly. The British intended to clarify authority relationships and consolidate their governance over these groups.[112]

One exception to the British policy of simply codifying existing practice was their attempt to formalize the grant of a hakura to the northern nomadic camel-herding groups because they had not been given one under the Fur Sultanate. Due in part to internal disagreements among the Abbala over who would be Nazir, or chief of the northern tribes, the Nazirship and land grant were never formalized. The absence of a legally granted Abbala homeland contributed to a different approach to land management and a sense of insecurity among the Abbala.[113] Flint and de Waal, based on interviews conducted in Darfur, state that "to this day, many *Abbala* Arabs explain their involvement in the current conflict in terms of the 250-year-old search for land, granted to the *Baggara*, but denied to them."[114]

The system of native administration did little to develop Darfur. By 1935, it had one elementary school and two "subgrade" schools. This was at least partly by design, as the colonial authorities feared the destabilizing effects of half-literate, discontented men who might challenge the authority of existing tribal chiefs.[116] Health systems were equally neglected, with no maternity clinic at all until the 1940s. At independence in 1956, Darfur had 0.57 hospital beds per thousand population, the lowest number of hospital beds of any Sudanese province. A railroad from Khartoum to Nyala in southern Darfur was completed in 1960, but there were no hard-surface roads connecting towns until the late 1970s.[117] Flint and de Waal note:

> When the first agro-economic studies were done in the 1960s, in preparation for two immense rural development schemes (the Western Savanna Development Corporation, based in Nyala, and the Jebel Marra Rural Development Project, based in Zalingei) the first researchers and planners found themselves in virgin developmental territory.[118]

Figure 6: Timeline of Governance Factors in the Darfur Conflict

	1630–1916	1917–1971	1971	1975–1982	1982–1984	1985–1986	1987–1989	1990–2003 escalation
Governance Factors in Build-up to the Conflict	Sultans governed through local elites Sultanate builds multi-ethnic province	Darfur under Tribal Administration system, first under British until 1956, then under Khartoum, relied on tribal chiefs to keep the peace and mediate conflicts	Native administration abolished, but Sudanese state fails to fill the institutional void for conflict mediation	Frequency of conflicts over water and grazing rights increases	Khartoum initially denies famine, which kills 100,000, and fails to respond or to mediate conflicts over water and grazing land	Conflicts associated with drought left unmediated and unresolved, hardening ethnic divisions	First Arab-Fur War	Key provisions of June 1989 Peace agreement not implemented 1994 Darfur gerrymandered into three states, reducing the Fur to a minority in each 2003 War and mass killings

Sources: Flint and de Waal (2008), Collins (2008), O'Fahey (2008), Bassil (2006)

What the system of native administration lacked in terms of development impetus, it made up for—in the eyes of those governing Darfur, at least—in terms of keeping order among tribal groups.[119] Perhaps for this reason, when Sudan gained its independence in 1956, the government initially continued the practice of tribal administration, with some adjustments.[120] The tribal chiefs' administrative powers were untouched, but their judicial powers were curtailed to a degree.[121] Thus, tribal administration contributed to Darfur's relative isolation from Sudanese institutions.[122] Then, in 1971, President Nimeiri abolished the native administration system entirely as part of his drive to "modernize" and remove the vestiges of colonialism, but the state institutions meant to take its place were completely ineffective.[123] This decision ultimately would prove a fateful one, as it undermined the authority of tribal chiefs but provided no effective institutional replacement. The ultimate result was that conflicts were allowed to fester.[124]

The table at Figure 7 includes data from a 2003 study by Bashar, published by the United Nations Environmental Program in 2007, cataloging major conflicts between tribal groups in Darfur, and their causes.[125] Three observations suggest themselves from the data. First, the tribal conflicts were preponderantly over grazing rights and water rights. Second, such conflicts were more frequent among nomadic groups than between settled groups and nomadic groups. Third, conflicts over grazing and water rights became more frequent in and after the 1970s, when rainfall levels began their decline in Darfur, and tend to cluster in and after years of drought, such as those that occurred in 1974–1975, 1982–1984, and 1990–1991. Before the 1971 abolition of the system of tribal administration, such conflicts were much rarer.

In a separate assessment of tribal conflicts, Harir cataloged 13 major local conflicts between 1957 and 1990 in which reconciliation conferences had taken place. Nine of the 13 conflicts involved pastoral Arab groups fighting each other over grazing and water rights or over animal theft, while the remaining four involved Arabs fighting non-Arabs.[126]

By and large, before 1971 such conflicts were kept from escalating out of control by tribal mechanisms. These included payment of blood money (*diyya*), material compensation, mediation by tribal chiefs or religious figures, or the holding of tribal conferences. Although they were less frequent, the fights between Arabs and non-Arabs had more potential for escalation; one

No.	Tribal groups involved	Year	Main cause of conflict
\multicolumn{4}{c}{Figure 7: Causes of Local Conflicts in Darfur from 1930 to 2000}
1	Kababish, Kawahla, Berti, and Medoub	1932	Grazing and water rights
2	Kababish, Medoub, and Zyadiya	1957	Grazing and water rights
3	Rezeigat, Baggara, and Maalia	1968	Local politics of administration
4	Rezeigat, Baggara, and Dinka	1975	Grazing and water rights
5	Beni Helba, Zyadiya, and Mahriya	1976	Grazing and water rights
6	Northern Rezeigat (Abbala) and Dago	1976	Grazing and water rights
7	N Rezeigat (Abbala) and Bargo	1978	Grazing and water rights
8	N Rezeigat and Gimir	1978	Grazing and water rights
9	N Rezeigat and Fur	1980	Grazing and water rights
10	N Rezeigat (Abbala) and Bargo	1980	Grazing and water rights
11	Taaisha and Salamat	1980	Local politics of administration
12	Kababish, Berti, and Ziyadiya	1981	Grazing and water rights
13	Rezeigat, Baggara, and Dinka	1981	Grazing and water rights
14	N Rezeigat and Beni Helba	1982	Grazing and water rights
15	Kababish, Kawahla, Berti, and Medoub	1982	Grazing and water rights
16	Rezeigat and Mysseriya	1982	Grazing and water rights
17	Kababish, Berti, and Medoub	1983	Grazing and water rights
18	Rezeigat and Mysseriya	1984	Grazing and water rights
19	Gimir and Fallata (Fulani)	1987	Administrative boundaries
20	Kababish, Kawahla, Berti, and Medoub	1987	Grazing and water rights
21	Fur and Bidayat	1989	Armed robberies
22	Arab and Fur	1989	Grazing, cross-boundary politics
23	Zaghawa and Gimir	1990	Administrative boundaries
24	Zaghawa and Gimir	1990	Administrative boundaries

No.	Tribal groups involved	Year	Main cause of conflict
	Figure 7: Causes of Local Conflicts in Darfur from 1930 to 2000, cont.		
25	Taaisha and Gimir	1990	Land
26	Bargo and Rezeigat	1990	Grazing and water rights
27	Zaghawa andMaalia	1991	Grazing and water rights
28	Zaghawa and Marareit	1991	Grazing and water rights
29	Zaghawa and Beni Hussein	1991	Grazing and water rights
30	Zaghawa, Mima, and Birgid	1991	Grazing and water rights
31	Zaghawa and Birgid	1991	Grazing and water rights
32	Zaghawa and Birgid	1991	Grazing and water rights
33	Fur and Turgum	1991	Land
34	Zaghawa and Arab	1994	Grazing and water rights
35	Zaghawa Sudan and Zaghawa Chad	1994	Power and politics
36	Masalit and Arab	1996	Grazing, administration
37	Zaghawa and Rezeigat	1997	Local politics
38	Kababish Arabs and Midoub	1997	Grazing and water rights
39	Masalit and Arab	1996	Grazing, administration
40	Zaghawa and Gimir	1999	Grazing, administration
41	Fur and Arab	2000	Grazing, politics, armed robberies

Source: UNEP (2007).

of the documented conflicts, in 1987–1989, escalated into a major ethnic war, involving 27 Arab tribes from across the region against the Fur. The first Fur-Arab war, as it was later termed, became a major factor in the escalation of the levels of violence.[127]

Flint and de Waal argue that as the authority of traditional tribal chiefs as moderating forces was eroded, the conflicts displayed a pattern of increasing polarization along ethnic lines. They cite a 1968 incident sparked by livestock theft between nomadic Zaghawa and Rizeigat Arabs; the leading families of the groups involved all had mixed heritage. After this incident, however, the Zaghawa, Kaitinga, and Tunjur ended their old practice of entrusting their camels to Arab herders, and Zaghawa herders took over care of the camels from Dor, the village in question.[128]

Edwards argues that by the 1980s and early 1990s, with a history of violent interaction between tribes vying for resources and no mechanisms to address the underlying disputes, the situation had become unmanageable. Indeed, in 1991, the Zaghawa tribe of Darfur pleaded to President Umar al-Bashir to address the breakdown in the social order, stating, "The Khartoum government has created a major crisis by meddling with the system of native administration."[129]

Climate Change and Desertification

Climate change exacerbated the governance challenges of mediating disputes in Darfur. Over the last decades, Darfur, and the Sahel more broadly, experienced long-term climate changes as well as extreme year-to-year climate variability. These long-term changes were:

(1) Sharp decline in annual rainfall levels beginning in 1971,

(2) Desertification, and

(3) Increased average temperatures.

The effects of these changes on Darfur's inhabitants were particularly acute in the north, the home of the camel-herding Abbala Arab clans, who did not have a land grant.

Rainfall Trend: As noted previously, rainfall in Darfur varies sharply by latitude across Darfur's three ecological zones, transitioning rapidly from the arid north, on the edge of the Sahara, to the subhumid tropical south. There is some disagreement in the academic literature about how best to characterize the long-term changes in precipitation patterns (see figures 8, 9, and 11). Most sources find that there has been a gradual reduction in average rainfall throughout the Sahel, as well as in Darfur. The UN Economic Program data (see figure 9) show a reduction of 16 to 34 percent in rainfall in different regions of Darfur, when comparing the period 1946–1975 to the 1976–2005 period.[130] Several others echo these basic conclusions. Rainfall is supplemented by groundwater withdrawals and use of seasonal watercourses

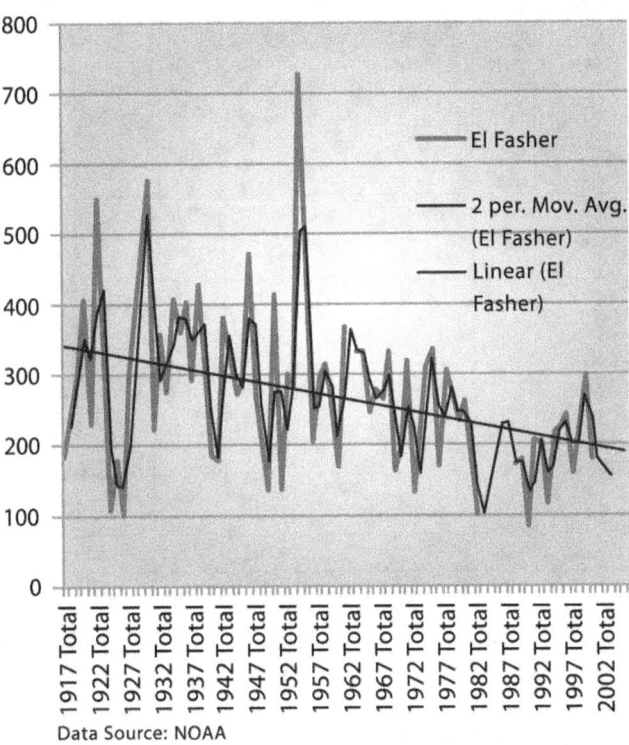

Figure 8. Annual Precipitation at el Fasher, Darfur

Data Source: NOAA

known as *wadis*. Abdalla identifies 12 wadis in Darfur, 3 in the north and 9 in the south.[131]

Kevane and Gray argue that, rather than continuous decline, the best characterization of the rainfall data is a structural break in the early 1970s across the Sahel, with rainfall varying around a new and lower average value after that period. Using the Kevane and Gray data, average rainfall at the four Darfur weather stations considered dropped 22.3 percent from the pre-1971 average rainfall of 424 millimeters, to 329.25 millimeters post-1971. Although the Kevane and Gray analysis of the precipitation data is not inconsistent with the UNEP and previous academic findings, it does differ significantly from most analyses in the interpretation of the effect of drought on the conflict, a point to which we will return later.[132]

Figure 9: Gauging the Rainfall Data									
Rainfall in Darfur					Rainfall Trends 1940–2002				
Rainfall Stations	Average annual rainfall (mm) 1946–1975	Average annual rainfall (mm) 1976–2005	Reduction (mm)	Percent Change	Year of break	Mean rainfall before 1971 (mm)	Mean rainfall after 1971 (mm)	Standard Deviat'n before break	Standard Deviat'n after break
Al Fasher, Northern Darfur	272.36	178.9	-93.46	-34%	1971	286	191	104	68
Nyala, Southern Darfur	448.71	376.5	-72.21	-16%	1970	459	362	95	89
El Geneina, Western Darfur	564.2	427.7	-136.5	-24%	1971	553	403	124	120
En Nahud	--	--	--	--	1965	398	361	94	100
Data Source: UNEP (2007)					**Data Source:** Kevane and Gray (2008)				

In addition to rainfall changes, Darfur experienced a decrease in the capacity of its water-supply system after 1970, as water works, ponds, and excavated water tanks were allowed to deteriorate through neglect. This deterioration was marked by reduced capacity to water livestock and sustain the human population.[133]

Desertification Trend: Desertification has been identified as a problem in Darfur, and Sudan more generally, since the 1950s; the edge of the Sahara advanced southward about 100 kilometers over a period of four decades.[134] This process is partly due to long-term climate changes experienced by the region, notably the substantial reduction in average precipitation. In the case of Darfur, desertification also has human causes, including deforestation, over-grazing, and overuse of water sources.[135] Population pressure may be a factor as well, but good demographic data are lacking.[136] The nomadic groups of northern Darfur, including the Abbala Arabs and the Zaghawa, have been the most affected by this process of desertification.[137] Desertification in the Sahel appears to have peaked in the 1980s, and satellite data suggest it may have halted or partially reversed in the 1990s.[138]

Figure 10: Timeline of Climate Factors in the Darfur Conflict							
	1956–1971	1971	1974–1975	1975–1982	1982–1984	1987–1989	1991
Major climate-related events	1950 – Desertification first identified as emerging problem in Northern Darfur, affecting the Abbala Arab camel herders. Desertification trend peaks in late 1980s.	Break in trend rainfall levels reduces mean rainfall by 33% in the north, 21% in the south.	Drought	Number of conflicts over water and grazing rights increases.	Major drought and famine with 100,000 dead; sharp conflicts over water and grazing with localized violence; economic losses deepen marginalizationof Abbala Arab nomads in north.	First Arab-Fur War, thousands killed, first appearance of Janjawiid. Proximate spark was spillover from Chadian civil war in already tense Darfur. Much of the violence focused on control of water sources and land for grazing and farming.	Drought and renewed conflicts over water sources

Sources: Flint and de Waal (2008), Collins (2008), O'Fahey (2008), Bassil (2006)

The 1982–1984 Drought and Famine

Temperature Trend: Temperature data reflect long-term changes as well. The IPCC reported there had been a 0.2- to 1-degree Celsius increase in average temperatures in the Sahel from 1970 to 2004.[139] The UNEP projects further temperature increases of between 0.5 Celsius and 1.5 degrees Celsius over the period 2030–2060.[140]

Along with longer-term climate trends, Darfur experiences significant inter-annual variability in precipitation. Notable recent droughts include

1974–1975, 1982–1984, and 1990–1991; the latter two droughts were also associated with famine. Rainfall variability remains high, although it may have declined slightly after 1970.[141] Darfurians were accustomed to dealing with such variability; their traditional lifestyles as desert nomads and settled farmers were complementary and well adapted to their environments. The traditional land use patterns, while occasionally contested, were generally accepted arrangements that served as an informal institutional framework in Darfur.[142]

This modus vivendi would be broken down, however, when the effects of the long-term climate changes described above combined with the climatic shock represented by the extreme drought and famine of 1982–1984. Long-term trends began to change the migration patterns of nomads as early as the 1970s, when nomadic herders from Chad, responding to these pressures, began crossing into western Darfur in greater numbers in search of water and pasture.[143] We noted above that the number of conflicts over water and grazing began to increase in the 1970s, as northern nomads adjusted their migration routes in search of water and pasture.[144] But the drought and famine of 1982–1984 proved to be a tipping point. The drought was severe. It accelerated the process of desertification in northern Darfur, and as a result, camel-herding Abbala nomads were forced in much larger numbers to change their migration routes southward, leading to significantly increased pressure on water and grazing

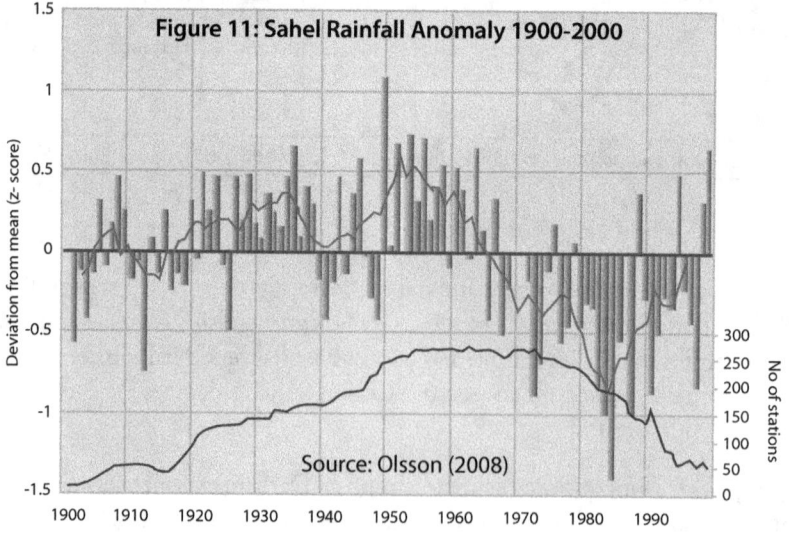

Figure 11: Sahel Rainfall Anomaly 1900-2000

Source: Olsson (2008)

resources in central and southern Darfur.[145] Some nomads attempted to settle and farm, exacerbating competition for land with existing farmers. Conflicts over wells and water sources, sometimes violent, resulted.[146]

Eighty percent of Darfur's population were employed in agriculture and related activities, which made the region vulnerable to the combination of long-term desertification and rainfall decline and the sharp shock of major drought.[147] Moreover, since niches of production, such as nomadism or sedentary agriculture, were aligned in many cases with ethnic identity, the climate-related disruptions carried the potential to escalate tensions along ethnic lines.[148]

The impacts of the 1982–1984 drought were particularly severe; the naturally more arid north was even harder hit than the south.[149] The average herd size of Darfur's pastoralists fell by 86 percent. In the south, 37 percent of the cattle were lost as compared to 71 percent in the north. The northern Abbala Bedouin camel-herders lost 70 percent to 90 percent of their herds. The losses deepened the Abbala's marginalization in Darfur. Grain and cereal production fell dramatically. Teklu et al. point out that the local markets for cereals and grains were very thin and highly responsive to production changes; the drought led to a 500 percent increase in these prices by 1985, as compared to 1980.[150] Death rates in Darfur tripled during 1982–1984 and as many as 100,000 Darfurians succumbed to either famine or disease.[151]

In 1985, Alex de Waal interviewed Sheikh Hilal Mohamed Abdala, the chief of the Rizeigat Abbala Arabs, whose son, Musa Hilal, later became the Nazir of the Janjawiid, at a moment when the far-reaching effects of the climate changes were becoming apparent:

> The proud old Sheikh ... spoke darkly of how the cosmic order was changing. In the old days, the nomads had been welcome guests of the Fur and Tunjur farmers. He himself had travelled south every year to Kargula on the slopes of Jebel Marra, where the Fur and the nomads would assist the farmers by buying their grain, taking their goods to market, and grazing their camels on the stubble of the harvest.... But now this was changing. Fur farmers were barring the Arabs' migratory routes and forcing camel herders to range

further south in search of pastures. The livestock migration route that began at Rahad Gineid now passed through Foro Baranga into southern Chad and the Central African Republic.... In the far north, in Wadi Howar, the Um Jalul shared the pastures with other herders, the Zaghawa and Meidob. But this too was changing. The famous *jizu* desert pastures had bloomed that year (1985) for the first time in seven years. Hilal brooded over the ecological changes that were disturbing the region. But he would rather die than change. For him, the old ways were the only ways.[152]

The 1982–1984 drought and famine served as the tipping point, however, as a series of conflicts over wells, wadis, and land (water and pasture) upset the previous balance in Darfur. Harir makes the case that the drought placed land tenure arrangements (known as *hakura*) in central Darfur, under unbearable stress.[153] The conflicts associated with the 1982–1984 drought, left unmediated and unresolved, divided populations into ethnic camps and hardened barriers between tribal groups, a process akin to radicalization along ethnic lines.[154] De Waal argues that "Darfurians showed extraordinary skill and resilience in surviving the famine of 1982–1984, but at the cost of drawing down their reserves of productive and social capital. Impoverishment and the undermining of community authority left Darfur vulnerable to conflict sparked by other factors."[155]

Although initially localized, the conflicts were to prove more intractable and widespread than those experienced in other such cases for three major reasons. First, as noted previously, Khartoum's 1971 derogation of the tribal administration system of self-government and failure to replace it with its own institutional infrastructure created a relative power vacuum in Darfur. Khartoum's administrative indifference to the region compounded the sense of anarchy during the famine.[156] Second, the region had become inundated with weapons, a byproduct of the use of western Darfur as a rear base by rebel groups fighting to overthrow the government of neighboring Chad. The weapons further undercut the ability of the elders to mediate conflicts before they escalated beyond the capability of traditional mechanisms to address.[157] A third major factor was the use of ideology to form conflict groups, to which we will turn next.

Conflict Group Formation

Events related to ideology, security, and politics formed conflict groups, and were significant factors in hardening the ethnic divisions and inflammation of the conflict. The first of these was a radical ideology of Arab suprema-cism, which first began to appear in Darfur in the early 1980s.[158] Initially dismissed as a fringe element, a group calling itself the "Arab Gathering" appeared on the scene around the time of regional elections in 1981. Using inflammatory and often racist language, they called for Arabs to be given a greater share of regional governmental positions, claiming that the *zurga* ("blacks") had governed Darfur for long enough.[159] In early 1982, gunmen dressed in military uniforms surrounded a market in Awal, then beat and robbed only the non-Arab market-goers; similar incidents took place else-where. Flint and de Waal describe the group's ideology as a "convergence of Arab supremacism and Islamic extremism." The group argued that only the Prophet Mohammed's descendants—which both the Baggara and Abbala Ju-hayna Bedouins of Darfur claim—could rightfully govern Darfur.[160]

In October 1987, the "Committee of the Arab Gathering" sent President Sadiq al-Mahdi an open letter, signed by 23 prominent Darfurian Arabs, de-manding an end to the "neglect of the Arab race" and the "denial" of govern-ment positions, threatening "catastrophe" and "dire consequences" if demands were not met. Although led by Darfurian Arabs, the Arab Gathering em-braced a radical ideology that was promoted in part by Libyan leader Muam-mar Qaddafi.[161] Despite the group's demands, Mahdi appointed a Fur as governor of Darfur. The Arab Gathering then published a directive to its members to "cripple" the new governor's administration, to "eliminate Fur leaders," disrupt agricultural production in Fur areas, and sow conflicts be-tween non-Arab tribes.[162] A second manifesto, published during the 1998–1999 period, contained significant detail on the group's objectives, and not-ed, among many ambitions, the importance of securing "sufficient pastures for nomads in Sudan, Chad, and the Central African Republic" and of their intention to kill all zurga.[163]

The ideology resonated with many Darfurian Arabs, given their historically marginalized position in Darfur and the increased precariousness of their livelihoods in light of desertification, drought, and a dearth of alternate economic opportunities. The Arab Gathering offered them a worldview, a cause, and a course of action to confront the forces purportedly holding them down.[164]

The Militia Strategy

In July 1985, Khartoum became alarmed at the unrest and sporadic violence in Darfur and implemented its "militia strategy," which involved the arming and use of local militia as proxies for fighting insurgency. This first use of Arab militia in Darfur was in response to an incursion of the Sudan People's Liberation Army (SPLA) into Kordofan Province, bordering on Darfur. The incursion alarmed Khartoum because the SPLA, which was fighting for independence in southern Sudan, previously had threatened to widen the war into northern Sudan.[165]

Because of poor governmental response to drought, Darfur was simmering with considerable discontent at this point. The riverine Arab elite in Khartoum, however, feared being pulled into fights on multiple fronts, and enlisted the ethnic Arab Baggara of southern Darfur to fight potential rebellion in Darfur on its behalf.[166] The president of the transitional government, General Abdel Rahman Suwar al-Dahab, dispatched his Minister of Defense, General Burma, to Kordofan and Darfur to arm and mobilize the Arab tribes against the SPLA. Burma selected former Arab army officers and Ansar (a militant Islamic movement) commanders to lead the Arab Baggara militias. Opting for militarized responses to deal with discontent, instead of political or economic solutions, would become Khartoum's default plan of action in Darfur. As Flint and de Waal explain:

> In return, the *Baggara* were promised a free hand to seize cattle and other possessions from the Dinka and Nuba populations suspected of supported the rebels. Known in official parlance as 'Friendly Forces' and locally as *Murahaliin*, these militias became synonymous with atrocity. They sprang into the public eye in April 1987, when more than one thousand displaced Dinkas were shot and burned to death in the town of el Da'ien in south-eastern Darfur in retaliation for a series of battles in which the SPLA killed many Rizeigat militiamen.... In Bahr el Ghazal in 1986–88,

in the Nuba mountains in 1992–1995, in Upper Nile in 1998–2003, and elsewhere on just a slightly smaller scale, militias supported by military intelligence and aerial bombardment attacked with unremitting brutality. Scorched earth, massacre, pillage, and rape were the norm.[167]

The arms given to the Baggara to fight the SPLA were later used against the Fur in the 1987–1989 Arab-Fur war.[168]

Chad, Weapons Proliferation, and the First Arab-Fur War (1987–1989)

Spillover from the conflict in neighboring Chad served also to radicalize the ethnic groups in Darfur, eventually providing the proximate spark of the 1987–1989 Arab-Fur war. Entanglements between Chad and Darfur go back a long way. As noted previously, several western districts of the Keira Sultanate were given over to French colonial government in 1917, districts that later became part of Chad. The population of these areas included several nomadic groups, including non-Arab Zaghawa camel-herders and several Bedouin Arab camel-herding groups, whose traditional ranges of migration straddled the new border. Politics crossed the border as well: Collins et al. note that the border areas of western Darfur have been the base for every overthrow of a Chadian regime since that country's independence.[169] In 1982, Hissene Habré, an ethnic Zaghawa whose rebel Forces Armées du Nord (FAN) included nomadic Zaghawa clans from both sides of the border, came to power in Chad after ousting Idriss Déby.[170]

With the change of power in Chad, many Arab nomadic groups in Chad who feared the non-Arab Habré regime began moving to western Darfur in significant numbers, beginning in 1983. Some lived in teeming refugee camps along the border, but two-thirds of the 27,000 refugees began to settle and farm among their ethnic kinsmen in Darfur. Armed Chadian opposition groups also crossed the border and settled among the refugees. Chadian Arab refugees were in an even more insecure and marginal position than Darfurian Arabs.[171]

After Sudanese President Nimeiri was overthrown in April 1985, the interim Sudanese government allowed Libya's Muammar Qadhafi to use Darfur as a rear base in support of the insurrection against Habré waged by Chadian

Figure 12: Timeline of Conflict Group Formation in the Darfur Conflict

1971–1981	1981–1984	1985	1987	1987–1989
Growing number of conflicts over water and grazing	**1981:** First signs of Arab Supremacist ideology emerge in Darfur. **1982:** Ethnic incident targeting non-Arabs at Awal **1982–1984:** Conflicts and localized violence associated with drought and famine	**April:** Overthrow of Nimeiri, opening of Darfur border with Libya, allowing weapons proliferation into Darfur. **July:** Given tense post-famine situation in Darfur, in Khartoum use of Baggara Arab militia as proxy to combat perceived threat of insurrection in South Darfur.	**October:** "Committee of the Arab Gathering," made up of 23 prominent Darfurian Arabs, demands an end to the "neglect of the Arab race" and threatens catastrophe if demands not met.	First Arab-Fur War, thousands killed, first appearance of Janjawiid. Proximate spark was spillover from Chadian civil war in already tense Darfur.

1990	1991	1992–1995	1996–1999	1998–2003
Khartoum launches Islamist project to rebuild its base of support, becomes vehicle for the Arab Supremacist ideology.	SPLA incursion into Darfur fought off by tribal Baggara Arab militia armed by Khartoum. Arab supremacist ideology spreads.	Conflict in Nuba mountains neighboring Darfur in which Khartoum uses tribal militias as proxies. Continued low-level violence throughout first half of 1990s.	Arab-Masalit War in Darfur leaves thousands dead as Janjawiid act in concert with Sudanese government forces. Growing disillusionment of Fur leaders with Khartoum as the Islamist movement fails to deliver development for Darfur.	Conflict in Upper Nile. Khartoum continues to arm Janjawiid. **2000:** Split of Islamist movement. **2003:** Armed Darfurian opposition groups SLA and JEM begin attacks on government targets.

Sources: Flint and de Waal (2008), Collins (2008), O'Fahey (2008), Bassil (2006)

Arabs, led by the ousted Idriss Déby.[172] As a result, Libyan weapons began flowing into Darfur for the Chadian Arabs, but also made their way to Sudanese Arab groups, notably the Baggara Beni Halba.[173]

Darfur at this point was only beginning to recover from the 1982–1984 drought and famine. Tensions were still extremely high, given the continuing government neglect of the simmering conflicts in the region, the failure of traditional tribal conflict mediation, and Khartoum's arming of Arab tribal militia groups.[174] The arrival in 1987 of thousands of Chadian Arab rebels supported by Qaddafi's "Islamic legion" troops sparked an Arab-Fur conflict that killed thousands.[175]

Sharif Harir details how the Chadian and Islamic Legion forces moved into the Fur areas of the Jebel Marra highlands because the terrain provided more protection from occasional raids by Chadian government troops.[176] The Chadian Arab rebels, however, brought their herds with them, entering farms for food and water and trampling crops along the way. According to Harir:

> Conflicts caused by the destruction of crops by Arab herds led quickly to mutual retaliatory acts and banditry—stealing from each other's herds, burning unharvested farms, burning pasture grass by the Fur and the Arabs, irrespective of whether these Arabs were Chadians or Sudanese. . . . Being under these pressures, the Fur decided to take action. They resorted to the mass burning of pasture fields with a view to forcing the Arabs to move to other pasture areas, and attempted to withhold access to sources of water and retaliated in kind when their livestock were stolen by Arabs. The Arabs started retaliating by burning Fur villages and farms, by uprooting trees from orchards, and destroying Fur farm equipment, such as water pumps, ploughs, and trucks. Sudanese Arab tribes, neighboring the Fur, came to assist their "brother Arabs" of Chad. The war soon took ideological and racist leanings which were heavily laden with tribal bigotry. Arab bands called *janjawiid* and *fursan* roamed Fur areas, burning villages, killing indiscriminately, and appropriating Fur property at will. The Arab *janjawiid* slaughtered anyone whose tribal identity was Fur or looked

like a Fur in complexion or facial appearance, whether on a highway or in a village. The Fur also started developing their own groups, the *Malishiyat* (militias) and responded in a similar manner.[177]

The arming of the Fur (by Chadian President Habré, himself a non-Arab Zaghawa) drew Darfurian Arab groups into the fight in support of their Chadian "ethnic kin." Ultimately, most of the Arab clans in Darfur joined the fight, quickly escalating the violence along ethnic lines.[178]

The Sudanese government of Sadiq al-Mahdi ignored the war for as long as it could, given its reluctance to confront Qadhafi over the activities of the Chadian rebels and "Islamic Legion" troops he sponsored. It dismissed reports of fighting in Darfur as armed banditry.[179] In June 1989, shortly before Mahdi was deposed, Khartoum at last sponsored a peace conference between the Fur and the various Arab tribes engaged in the fighting. Intriguingly, the participants seemed to agree on one point: that the war was primarily about water and land. The Sudanese government representative's opening address to the conference stated:

> The conflict we are trying to resolve today began as an ordinary conflict between nomadic pastoralists and sedentary framers over natural resources. The extraordinary aspect of the Fur/Arabs conflict is not the manner in which it began, but the speed with which it spread out from the Jebel Marra areas to engulf communities in Wadi Salih, Zalingei, Kas, Kabkabiya, and Nyala rural council areas. The reckless use of firearms to ruthlessly massacre our peaceful citizens and the macabre mutilations are completely out of character with the people of Darfur.[180]

The Fur delegation's opening statement noted the conflict began as an "economic war," which, given the agricultural economy of Darfur, meant war over land and water sources. The Fur also noted the escalation of the war was on a "genocidal course" with the aim of "complete annihilation of the Fur people." The Fur claimed 2,500 of their people had been killed, 400 villages burned, and 40,000 head of livestock stolen, while the Arab side claimed 500 deaths and 3,000 livestock lost.[181] The participants' expressed view that the war had been primarily about land and water may have been a somewhat narrow one, given the role of Chadian Arab rebel groups as a spark; but it escalated, and did so along ethnic lines, in part because of the unresolved and unmediated conflictual inheritance of the 1982–1984 drought and famine. Those conflicts had likewise pitted Arab against Fur and left the region's tribal conflict mediation mechanisms exhausted when no central government relief came.

The conference did reach a negotiated peace deal, the same week that Umar al-Bashir seized power as Sudanese president.[182] Key provisions of the agreement called for the deportation of the Chadian militias and the disarming of the Fur militia—armed in part by Chadian President Habré—and the Arab "Janjawiid."[183] (The agreement was the first official use of the term *Janjawiid*.) Flint and de Waal note: "But the peace deal was not implemented, and politics in Darfur continued to polarize."[184]

Failures of the "paralyzed" central and regional governments to implement the peace agreement, according to Harir, completely undermined their credibility and worsened relations between ethnic groups.[185] In a similar vein, O'Fahey argues that, after Bashir took power in 1989, the conflicts displayed what he described as a growing "ethnicization."[186]

Conflict Interspersed with Violence, Punctuated by Failed Peace: 1990–2003

The failure to implement the 1989 peace agreement would collude with the growing strength of Arab supremacists in Khartoum and Darfur to make conflict and violence Darfur's constant companion over the next decade and a half.

Bashir's new government, strongly supported by the National Islamic Front (NIF), embraced the Arab Supremacist ideology being promoted by Qaddafi that began permeating the region. Key figures of the NIF began to support the racist project of some Darfurian Arabs to supplant the non-Arab groups in Darfur. They overcame some class contradictions in doing so, as Nureldine points out: "There is hardly any connection, for instance, between the 'Arabs' of riverine Sudan and those of Darfur. Indeed, if the former are associated with privilege and power, the latter are the most wretched of the Darfuri population."[187] That wretchedness, however, made the Darfurian Arabs more susceptible to manipulation by radicals. In the words of one of the refugees who fled the ethnic cleansing: "When the new Islamic government came to power in Sudan in the early 1990s, they prepared Arab tribes to kill African tribes in western Sudan. . . . [T]he government of Sudan wants to kill Darfurians and replace them with Arabs."[188]

Many Fur Islamists initially supported the National Islamic Front, hoping that it would promote development in Darfur and that, as fellow Muslims, non-Arab groups would receive fairer treatment than they had previously. Instead, they were systematically excluded from power. Thus, when the Islamists split in 1999, most non-Arab Darfurian Islamists went into the opposition.[189] Per Flint and de Waal: "Beneath this power struggle was an ethnic-regional split: the Islamist *securitate* joined with the traditional riverine military elite to create a security cabal at the heart of the Sudanese state. There were no Darfurians in the inner circle."[190]

In 1990–1991, another drought and famine hit Darfur. As occurred during the 1982–1984 drought and famine, the government did little to ease the situation, leading to "growing anger in the population."[191] Once again, as nomadic groups were forced to alter their migration patterns, they came into renewed conflict with settled farmers over land for pasture and water sources. This time, the violence included reprisals for atrocities that took place during the 1987–1989 Arab-Fur conflict.[192]

In 1991, the SPLA again attempted an incursion into Darfur from southern Sudan in order to widen its war against the government. SPLA forces under Daud Bolad entered Southern Darfur. Khartoum once again used its "militia strategy"; the SPLA forces were routed by the Baggara Arab Beni Halba and several villages suspected of having harbored the SPLA were burned. Although the Baggara Arab militia did fight the SPLA on behalf of Khartoum, and engage in atrocities while doing so, the Baggara would later refuse to participate in Khartoum's militia strategy to suppress dissent among the Fur, Masalit, and non-Arab Darfurians.[193]

In 1994, as part of a constitutional reform, Darfur was divided into three administrative districts. Gerrymandering reduced the Fur to a small minority in each of the three new districts, depriving them of their previous administrative power. This was followed by attempts to reform the old hakura system of land tenure, in order to undermine the land holdings of non-Arab groups. These actions predictably caused unrest, to which Khartoum responded by arming more proxies, notably the Janjawiid, primarily composed of Abbala nomads from northern Darfur.[194]

Several violent incidents also occurred between the nomadic Abbala Arab groups and the nomadic non-Arab Zaghawa, both camel-herding groups. In 1991, a fight over water access at Rahad Ginied left fifteen Zaghawa dead. In a 1992 incident, the government allowed armed Arab nomads from Chad to access Darfur in the Abu Gamra area, a violation of the 1989 peace agreement that ended the Fur-Arab war. In 1994, two trucks carrying twenty-seven Zaghawa were stopped close to Kutum and seventeen of the Zaghawa were killed.[195] Several Zaghawa were killed in a land and grazing dispute with the Aulad Zeid in 2001. These incidents were symptomatic of the low-level violence that Darfurians experienced for at least two decades. The Zaghawa would later fight the Janjawiid with the Fur.[196]

From 1996–1998, the Janjawiid targeted the Masalit in what some researchers have labeled the "Arab-Masalit" war. The Masalit are, like the Fur, a non-Arab tribe engaged in sedentary agriculture in central Darfur. Beginning in 1996, the government imprisoned and tortured Masalit leaders, while Masalit communities were subjected to systematic attacks. As many as 2,000 Masalit were killed, hundreds of villages were burned, and an estimated 100,000 Masalit fled to neighboring Chad.[197] The government coordinated its actions with the Janjawiid,

"I saw them take fifty-two men from my village, including my cousin, and they took them to the edge of the mountain, made them go on their knees, put the gun in their mouths, and shot each one of them."—Statement of a survivor to a U.S. investigation team at refugee camp in Chad.

J. Hagan and W. Rymond-Richmond, *Darfur and the Crime of Genocide* (2008).

using army troops to disarm villagers a few days before Janjawiid attacks. The Masalit would become allies of the Fur resistance groups that emerged to public view in 2003.[198]

The National Islamic Front split in 2000 added to Khartoum's fear of insurrection in Darfur, as many Fur Islamists joined the opposition. In response, the government stepped up its arming of the proxy militia and began disarming non-Arabs.[199] The Janjawiid began their offensive against the Fur in earnest in October 2002, with attacks in South Darfur. By 2003, the Janjawiid had already killed 160 civilians and burned hundreds of villages, with complete impunity. In 2002, the Fur began formally to organize their armed resistance movements, with many Fur Islamists joining the Justice and Equality Movement (JEM) and others the Sudan Liberation Army (SLA).[200]

In February and March 2003, the two armed Fur opposition groups, JEM and SLA, publicly announced their existence and published manifestos. Soon after, in April 2003, they began attacking targets such as the al Fasher airport, using guerilla-style tactics. The Janjawiid, in coordination with the Sudanese government and supported by government troops and aircraft, began a counteroffensive in July of the same year. In the ensuing conflict, the Janjawiid engaged in mass rape and killings rape of Fur villagers.[201] These actions were declared to be a case of genocide by U.S. Secretary of State Colin Powell, in September 2004 testimony to the U.S. Congress.[202] The conflict resulted in the deaths of an estimated 300,000 people and displaced over 2.7 million people.[203]

How Did It Happen?

As we have seen, the two decades before the point when the Darfur conflict emerged into the international community's collective consciousness in 2003 were violent ones in Darfur. Periods of heavier fighting, such as the 1982–1984 drought, the 1987–89 Fur-Arab war, the April 1987 massacre of the Dinka in southeastern Darfur, the 1991 drought, a 1991 SPLA incursion, and the 1996–1998 Arab-Masalit conflict, were interspersed with periods of lower-level violence. However, they were all part of the same set of processes. Violence, initially localized, started with the inability of locals to deal with the 1982–1984 drought and famine, the severity of which brought to the fore the hitherto background effects of longer-term climate change. Nureldine, among other scholars, argues that the initial driving force of the conflict was not ethnic identity, "but a search for land in an ecological crisis.... Whoever controlled the land would survive the crisis; the loser would perish."[204] Although there is little doubt that conflict over land and water was the initial force driving the conflict, several other major factors combined to ensure that the conflict escalated and radicalized participants along ethnic lines. These were

(1) The lack of effective mediation of the initial conflicts, as the institutional vacuum encouraged groups to take matters into their own hands;

(2) Spill-over from the Chad conflict and the North-South conflict in Sudan, including weapons proliferation, which undermined the authority of tribal elders; and

(3) A radical ideology of Arab supremacism.

Flint and de Waal quote a saying in Darfur that "conflict defines origins."[205] The severe drought and famine in 1982–1984 thrust competing groups into sometimes-violent conflict over water and resources. The failure of conflict resolution mechanisms and government neglect allowed these conflicts to fester, radicalizing groups along ethnic and tribal lines. Had there been an effective governmental response in 1982–1984, both in terms of relief for the famine and mediation of the disputes, the escalation likely would not have occurred. But Sudan's weak and illegitimate government felt threatened by the simmering discontent and low-level violence in Darfur, feared spillover from the war with the South, and elected instead to suppress discontent in Darfur using its Arab tribal militia proxies. The Arab supremacist ideology that arrived in Darfur in the 1980s found adherents, particularly among members of the marginalized and poor Abbala nomadic Arabs. The 1986–1987 opening of the borders to Chadian rebels and Qadhafi's "Islamic Legion" then proved the proximate spark that set off generalized violence, spanning the period 1987–1989. Thousands were killed; the conflict was witness to mass killings and burning of villages and crops. The 1991 drought and famine, while not as severe as the 1982–1984 version, witnessed renewed violent conflicts over water and land, with many tribes engaging in retributions for atrocities that took place during the 1987–1989 Arab-Fur war. By then, however, conflict startup condition—following on Sandole—had been reached, and events had become prisoners of the logic of escalation, retribution, and radicalization, leading to the point at which the conflict broke into the international consciousness in 2003.[206]

Perhaps the most interesting question is whether the climate changes and the 1982–1984 drought and famine were a necessary condition for the subsequent wars. The very severe drought (and broader climate changes, including desertification) had a particularly polarizing effect because the ensuing conflicts pitted ethnic groups against each other for survival. This activated previously latent ethnic divisions, while tensions went unmediated and unresolved. The 1987–1989 Arab-Fur conflict escalated quickly from relatively small-scale conflicts over water and land, in part because of those ethnic divisions, which were exploited by the growing Arab Supremacist movement. It is difficult to imagine another event with a similar and equally severe ethnically polarizing effect as the drought within the context of this region. If the drought was a necessary condition, however, it alone was not a sufficient condition for the localized violence to become widespread and organized. That required the failure of mediation mechanisms and the spread of the introduction of the Arab Supremacist ideology.

Structural Factors in the Background of the Conflict

In addition to the environmental, governance, and ideological processes discussed above, several broad structural political and economic attributes of Sudan likely played indirect roles in the escalation of the Darfur conflict from the first outbreaks of localized violence. These are worth highlighting for their potential applicability to a broader range of cases.

State Legitimacy/Fragility: Sudan may be the poster child of state fragility and lacks legitimacy among the groups it governs. It gained independence in 1956 and inherited a set of boundaries with little connection to the historical states that had previously occupied that geography. The three distinct regions where separate processes of state formation had been occurring—Darfur, the Nile valley, and the South—were joined into one nation-state, on the Westphalian model, by conquest and the decisions of colonial Britain.[207] Darfur, Kordofan, and the southern reaches of Sudan were included in this entity despite their history of independence; but the new Sudan lacked, and continues to lack, legitimacy among many of these groups.[208]

Figure 13: Combined Timeline of Darfur Conflict Factors

	1971	1972–1982	1982–1984	1985–1986	1987–1989	1990–2003 (Escalation)
Manifest Conflict and Conflict Group Formation		Frequency of conflicts over water and grazing increases	Radical ideology of Arab supremacism begins to appear in Darfur	April 1985: overthrow of Nimeiri. July 1985: Khartoum arms Baggara tribal militia as proxy to fight unrest in southern Darfur. Weapons proliferate as Chadian rebels begin using Darfur as rear base	First Arab-Fur War; thousands killed, first appearance of Janjawiid. Proximate spark was spillover from Chadian civil war in already tense Darfur. Much of the violence focused on control of water sources and land for grazing and farming	Key provisions of June 1989 peace agreement not implemented 1990–1991 Renewed drought. 1990 Khartoum launches "Islamist" project to rebuild its base of support, becomes vehicle for the Arab Supremacist ideology. 1991 SPLA incursion into Darfur. Continued low-level violence throughout first half of 1990s. Arab supremacist ideology spreads. 1992–1995 Conflict in Nuba mountains neighboring Darfur in which Khartoum uses tribal militias as proxies. 1994 Darfur gerrymandered into three states, reducing the Fur to a minority in each. Late 1990s Escalation of violence
Contributing Factors Governance	System of Native Administration abolished	Authority of tribal chiefs erodes, but Sudanese state fails to fill the institutional void for conflict mediation	Khartoum initially denies famine, does not mount adequate relief effort	Conflicts associated with drought left unmediated and unresolved, hardening ethnic divisions		
Foundation Natural Factors	Sharp reduction in average rainfall levels; desertification trend in north	Nomads forced to range further for water and grazing	Major drought and famine with 100,000 dead; sharp conflicts over water and			

Figure 13: Combined Timeline of Darfur Conflict Factors, cont.					
1971	1972–1982	1982–1984	1985–1986	1987–1989	1990–2003 (Escalation)
		grazing with localized violence; losses deepen marginalization of Abbala Arab nomads in north			1995–1999 Arab-Masalit war in Darfur leaves thousands dead as Janjawiid act in concert with Sudanese government forces

Growing disillusionment of Fur leaders with Khartoum as the Islamist movement fails to deliver development for Darfur

1998–2003 Conflict in Upper Nile

Perceiving the growing unrest in Darfur, in December 2002, Vice President Osman warns Darfur not to try to imitate the rebellion of the South

February–March 2003 Armed Darfurian opposition groups SLA and JEM begin attacks on government targets |

Sources: Flint and de Waal (2008), Collins (2008), O'Fahey (2008), Bassil (2006)

This lack of legitimacy across ethnic groups is likely one reason Khartoum so consistently opted for militarized responses to discontent in Darfur, instead of pursuing political solutions that would have required buy-in from the Fur and other Darfurian ethnic groups.

Economic Weakness: Economic weakness and questionable economic policy priorities may have exacerbated aspects of the Darfur conflict. Murshed notes the finding in the conflict prevention literature that inequality among ethnic groups, termed "horizontal inequality," is a major contributor to conflict, but data on such inequality are difficult to come by, as weak and failing governments often do not collect these data.[209] It is intriguing to consider that point in light of the distribution—in May 2000, outside mosques in Khartoum—of a volume titled *The Black Book: Imbalance of Power and Wealth in Sudan* by a group calling itself "Seekers of Truth and Justice." The *Black Book* documented the domination of economic and political power by the three tribes of the north Nile Sudan—the Shaygiyaa, Ja'Aliyiin, and Dangla—and the relative deprivation of other ethnic groups. The "seekers," according to Flint and de Waal, were members of the National Islamic Front who had lost patience with the NIF's failure to look past ethnic and tribal differences.[210]

The economic development strategy pursued by the Khartoum government is blamed by many observers for exacerbating regional disparities and favoring certain ethnic groups. What development resources the government had were spent on a few large-scale agriculture projects dedicated to export crops, such as sugar or cotton, rather than on projects that would increase the productivity in traditional sectors. While such plantation projects earned valuable foreign exchange, they created only a relative handful of jobs and displaced the small-holding farmers to marginally productive areas.[211] Income inequality was worsened by Sudanese economic policy, which led to hyperinflation and food shortages.[212]

Nielsen argues that monetization of the economy and the changes in economic relationships took place in a way that reinforced barriers between ethnic groups. The Nile Arab elite, known as *Jellaba*, monopolized capital and finance in Sudan. The traditional Fur economy, however, was built on land tenure arrangements for which there was no legal title, informal exchange of labor rather than market mechanisms, and personal relationships. As a result, the Fur spurned wage labor, limiting their ability to integrate into the emerging market-based economy.[213] In addition, as Barth notes, the Jellaba Arabs had become the buyers of agricultural commodities, and disagreements or "conflicts of interest between buyers and sellers are thus readily cast in ethnic terms and become politically loaded."[214] The failure of state and market mechanisms to ease the drought-induced famine of 1982–1984, moreover, led to increased emphasis on scarce land for survival.[215]

The lack of economic alternatives to agricultural activities, both nomadic and sedentary, for livelihoods in Darfur exacerbated the consequences of the environmental changes that occurred in Darfur. The Abbala Arabs had few options other than camel herding, particularly given the level of education in Darfur. Some emigrated to the Persian Gulf as laborers, but alternatives within Sudan were scarce.[216]

Could It Have Been Prevented?

From the point of view of conflict prevention, two observations about the Darfur conflict stand out. The first is about mediation. When it became independent, Sudan initially continued the British practice of using tribal chiefs to govern their people and maintain the peace on behalf of the state. The system was removed by Nimeiri in 1971, but, by and large, Sudanese institutions lacked the wherewithal or desire to fill the power vacuum. When Darfur's climate changed, beginning in the 1970s, nomadic groups were forced to adapt by changing their migration patterns. Sudanese institutions, however, did not effectively mediate the ensuing conflicts over water and land. Tribal chiefs attempted to fill the vacuum, but their efforts no longer had administrative or legal authority, and the influx of weapons led to rapid escalation when violence did break out. Had Sudanese institutions effectively dealt with land and water conflicts that emerged from climate change in Darfur, the ensuing escalation and radicalization along ethnic lines likely would have been averted.

The second point is that the Darfur conflict did not start as an ethnic war. The initial farmer-herder conflicts that kicked off the violence were about preserving livelihoods in the face of drought and famine. The conflict came to have an ethnic character for several reasons, notably the breakdown in traditional conflict resolution mechanisms (and their non-replacement with state institutions), the use of tribal militia as state proxies (which began as early as 1985), the spread of the radical ideology of Arab supremacism, the actions of conflict entrepreneurs (such as Musa Hilal) who fomented divisions to pursue narrow agendas of power grabbing, and Chadian national groups launching from Darfur.

These two observations also point to two key points in which early outside intervention could have affected the evolution of the conflict. Had the international community possessed a clear picture of the severity of the drought, relief efforts could have been mounted that could have helped avert the ensuing conflicts over water sources and land. Even after the drought and first Arab-Fur war, the window for effective structural conflict prevention arguably remained through the early 1990s. Development assistance by the international community to build wells and restore the degrading water infrastructure in Darfur could have helped avert the escalation of tensions and radicalization that took place in the 1990s. Such a development-oriented intervention would have created an opportunity to help restore the eroded conflict mediation authority of local leaders and undermined the ability of conflict entrepreneurs to create their pernicious narratives of exclusion.

Opposing View on Rainfall and Conflict in Darfur

There is one notable dissent in the academic literature from the view that rainfall and drought played an important part in the Darfur conflict that is worth addressing here. Kevane and Gray take an opposing view of the effect of rainfall in the Darfur conflict. They argue that there is only a weak relationship between climate change, specifically rainfall patterns, and the outbreak of the 2003 conflict. Based on a statistical analysis of rainfall patterns, they find that there was a break in the rainfall trend around 1971, instead of a continuing decrease in rainfall levels. While they acknowledge that the post-1971 average has fallen, they see little merit in the idea that it had anything to do with the 2003 conflict. In their words:

> Rainfall in Darfur did not decline significantly in the years immediately prior to the crisis. Furthermore, short-term but significant droughts in 1984 and 1990 did not provoke wide-spread conflict. As for the assertion that long-term

rainfall decline has led to the crisis, there is no evidence of a downwards trend. Instead, rainfall in Darfur exhibited a flat trend, though with high variability, in the thirty years preceding the conflict (1972–2002).[217]

The Kevane and Gray analysis, however, fails to look deeply enough into the historical record. As outlined in this chapter, the 1982–1984 drought brought to the fore the long-term effects of climate changes beginning in the 1970s; it was accompanied by conflicts, some violent, over water and land. Although the violence initially was not widespread, the conflicts it engendered, coupled with the failure of conflict resolution mechanisms (tribal and government), governmental neglect, spill-over from the war in Chad, and a racist ideology, combined to kick off two decades of violence, punctuated by the occasional peace agreement or lull to lower levels of conflict. As the United Nations Economic Program notes, Darfur has seen low-level violence for a "generation."[218]

Kevane and Gray also question the way some have used the finding in Miguel et al. that links droughts with an increased risk of outbreaks of violence in the subsequent year.[219] Kevane and Gray state that "the study was clear that, only as rainfall changes were mediated via incomes, would there be a reasonable empirical basis for linking rainfall to conflict."[220] There is no systematic data on how the 1982–1984 drought and famine affected incomes, but there nevertheless are sound reasons to think of the drought in terms of an economic shock. Teklu documented the extreme effects of the drought on agricultural production: the average herd size of Darfur's pastoralists fell by 86 percent; production of grain and sorghum also dropped dramatically.[221] Since 80 percent of the population was dependent on agriculture for livelihoods, it is clear there was a large, albeit unquantified, income shock for the majority of the population. As de Waal argues, one of the most significant impacts of the famine was the loss of productive assets (camel livestock) by the Abbala, which deepened their poverty and marginalization within Darfur.[222] In addition, other studies, such as Hendrix and Glazer, have replicated the finding of a relationship between rainfall variability and subsequent conflict, using models that did not depend on a link to incomes.[223]

Darfur in the Context of Global Climate Change

In June 2007, United Nations Secretary General Ban Ki-moon wrote an editorial that suggested that global climate change played a role in the outbreak of conflict in Darfur in 2003.[224] A few weeks before that, the mainstream news media had begun making similar points; writing in *The Atlantic* in 2007, Stephan Faris stated, "If [Darfur's] collapse was in some part caused by the emissions from our factories, power plants, and automobiles, we bear some responsibility for the dying."[225]

So what of the link to global climate change? Mr. Ban's editorial alluded to climate studies that linked the pattern of desiccation in the Sahel over the period of 1930–2000 to changes in ocean surface temperatures in the Indian Ocean. Based on global climate models, two studies by Gianini et al. found that Indian Ocean surface temperature variations were able to account for 60 percent of the observed rainfall changes in the Sahel over the 70-year period, and explain 25 percent to 35 percent of the interannual variation in rainfall.[226] The role of global climate change and anthropogenic greenhouse gases in increasing Indian Ocean temperatures is well established by several other studies, and is also one of the basic conclusions of the IPCC's work. However, Gianini noted that more work needs to be done to prove a direct connection.[227] In addition, oceanic influences are only part of the equation.

Ban Ki-moon's characterization of how climate changes and drought led to the conflict, however, leaves something to be desired. Mr. Ban states, "For the first time in memory, there was no longer enough food and water for all. Fighting broke out. By 2003, it evolved into the full-fledged tragedy we witness today."[228] While no doubt constrained by the necessity to be brief in a short editorial, Mr. Ban's characterization omits major factors that facilitated the escalation of what initially were localized conflicts. A second quibble is that while the 1982–1984 drought was very severe and clearly played a part in the genesis of the conflict, it is not possible to attribute a discrete weather event to the overall global process of climate change, even though it is evident that Darfur's climate was undergoing long-term changes. Regardless of the causes of the climate changes that Darfur has experienced, the role of those changes in the conflict was a significant one.

Finally, it is important to point out that acknowledging the role of environmental factors in the Darfur conflict does not imply that the Khartoum regime or the tribal militias should be held any less responsible for their actions. Had Khartoum fulfilled its responsibilities to its Darfurian population during the drought and famine of 1982–1984, the Sudanese government could have headed off the first stage of the process that led to conflict. Khartoum's consistent preference for militarized responses to the discontent that its own institutional failures caused, likewise, is complicit in the escalation of the conflicts. Its guilt for the organization, arming, and management of the Janjawiid is overwhelming.

Full Darfur Timeline

1630–1916	Darfur as an independent sultanate, the Keira Sultanate, centered on Dor, in the northern Jebel Mara highlands of Darfur.
1787	Darfur conquers Kordofan.
1821	Egyptian conquest of the Sudanese Nile.
1874	Overthrow of the Keira Sultanate of Darfur.
1884	Mahdists take control of Darfur.
1898	Defeat of the Mahdists and restoration of the Keira Sultanate.
1913	Drought and famine.
1916	Overthrow of Sultan Ali Dinar and incorporation of Darfur into Sudan.
1917–1956	Darfur under British rule as part of Sudan. Most people of Darfur begin process of cultural assimilation into the Sudanese entity, first under British, then under independent government.
1956	Sudan independence from Britain (with Darfur).
1960	Railway reaches Nyala in southern Darfur.
1966	Chadian opposition front FROLINAT founded in Nyala.
1967 or 1968	Incident of ethnic violence at Rahad Gineid sparked by accusation of livestock theft. This led to three days of violent encounters among Zaghawa and Abbala Arab herders, primarily Rizeigat. After this, the Zaghawa, Kaitinga, and Tunjur end their previous practice

of entrusting their camels to the Abbala Arabs, giving them instead into the care of Zaghawa camel herders.

1969	Jaafar Nimeiri takes power in Sudan.
1970	Ansar and Muslim Brothers flee Sudan.
1971	Native Administration system abolished. It had served as a dispute resolution forum, mitigating tribal conflicts.
1973	Libya begins smuggling weapons to Chadian opposition through Darfur.
1974–1975	Major drought.
1976	Ansar–Muslim Brothers invasion of Sudan from Libya.
1980	A regional government and elected governor provided for Darfur.
1982	Habré takes power in Chad.
1982–1984	Great drought and famine in Darfur; 100,000 dead and sharp conflicts over water and land for grazing.
April 1985	Overthrow of Nimeiri; opening of Darfur-Libya border.
July 1985	Sudanese regime begins using local Baggara Arab militias led by former army personnel to fight an incipient insurgency in Darfur.
1986	Omer sets up Chadian armed camps in Darfur.
1986–1989	Sadiq al-Mahdi government.
1986–1988	Conflict in Bahr el Ghazal, immediately south of Darfur; militias supported by military intelligence and aerial bombardment attacked civilians and burned villages.
1987–1989	First Arab-Fur war in Darfur in which thousands killed and hundreds of villages burned; Janjawiid first organized.
April 1987	One thousand Dinkas were shot and burned to death in the town of el Da'ien in southeastern Darfur in retaliation for a series of battles in which the SPLA killed many Rizeigat Arab militiamen.
June 1989	Inter-tribal conference reaches peace deal.
June 1989	President Bashir seizes power, with the initially covert support of the National Islamic Front (NIF).
1990	Beginning of severe drought in Darfur.

1990	Khartoum launches Islamist "civilization project" to build an Islamist constituency. Islamist cadres dispatched to villages to foment Islamist consciousness. Islamist philanthropic organizations mobilized to open schools and clinics and to support the popular defense forces.
December 1990	Chadian rebels led by Deby defeat Habré in Chad, with Sudanese and Libyan support. This cements the Chadian-Arab linkage to Khartoum, including support against the rebels in Darfur.
1991	Darfur becomes a state within a federal system.
December 1991	SPLA incursion in Darfur.
1992–1995	Conflict in the Nuba mountains; militias supported by military intelligence and aerial bombardment attack civilians.
1994	Darfur gerrymandered into three states; native administration reintroduced.
1995	Ali Osman becomes Foreign Minister.
March 1995	Nine amirs appointed for the Arabs in western Darfur.
1995	Sudanese-backed militants attempt to assassinate Egyptian President Mubarak during a visit to Addis Ababa.
1995–1999	Arab-Masalit conflict.
1998–2003	Conflict in the Upper Nile; militias supported by military intelligence and aerial bombardment.
May 2000	Distribution of *The Black Book: Imbalance of Power and Wealth in Sudan* outside mosques in Khartoum by a group calling itself "Seekers of Truth and Justice." The book documents the domination of economic and political power by the three tribes of the north Nile Sudan: the Shaygiyaa, Ja'Aliyiin, and Dangla. The "Seekers" were disaffected members of the Islamic movement in Sudan and disillusioned by the failure of the Islamic movement to look past tribal and ethnic differences.
2001	Organization of armed opposition in Darfur. (July 21, a group of Zaghawa and Fur resistance members met in Gamra and agreed to fight together against the Arab supremacist groups.)
2002	Conferences at Nyertete and Kas to try to mediate the conflict.

December 2002	Vice President Ali Osman warns Darfur not to follow the path of the South.
February 2003	SLA declares its existence and publishes manifesto.
March 2003	JEM declares its existence.
April 2003	Rebels attack el Fasher airport.
May 2003	Rebel attacks on Kutum, Mellit, Tine.
July 2003	Janjawiid counteroffensive begins.
September 2003	Government-SLA ceasefire talks in Abeche, Chad.
January 2004	Major government offensive.
March 2004	UN Coordinator Mukesh Kapila calls Darfur the world's worst humanitarian crisis and compares it to Rwanda.
April 2004	Government–SLA/JEM talks in N'djamena agree on a ceasefire and disarmament of the Janjawiid.
June 2004	U.S. Congress describes Darfur as a case of "genocide."
July 2004	UN Security Council gives Khartoum 30 days to disarm the Janjawiid and facilitate humanitarian assistance.
August 2004	Government and rebels hold talks in Abuja, Nigeria.
September 2004	U.S. Secretary of State Colin Powell declares Darfur to be a case of "genocide": the UN Security Council sets up an Independent Commission of Inquiry into Darfur (ICID).
January 2005	ICID report. Comprehensive peace agreement signed between Sudanese government and southern Sudan's SPLM in Nairobi, Kenya.
July 2005	Government of Sudan, SLA/M, and JEM sign Declaration of Principles in Abuja.
2009	The International Criminal Court indicts President Umar al-Bashir for war crimes and crimes against humanity.

Source: Flint and de Waal (2008), Collins (2008), O'Fahey (2008), Bassil (2006).

Chapter Four

From Climate Change to Conflict

Pathways from Climate Change to Conflict

The Darfur conflict outlined in the last chapter illustrates the role that climate change and climatic shocks can play in creating the potential for conflicts when they collude with other factors, especially in weak and failing states. This chapter attempts to put those findings within a broader framework, in order to draw lessons that may be applied elsewhere. These lessons include insights into the process by which climate change may lead to conflict, and the risk factors that play a part. This chapter develops a rough vulnerability screen based on these risk factors and describes the role of migration in such potential conflicts.

To illustrate the potential paths from climate changes to violent conflict, this chapter puts forth a basic model

> "*Happy families are all alike; every unhappy family is unhappy in its own way.*"
>
> Leo Tolstoy, *Anna Karenina*, Chapter 1, first line.

Figure 14: Model of Steps from Climate Change to Conflict

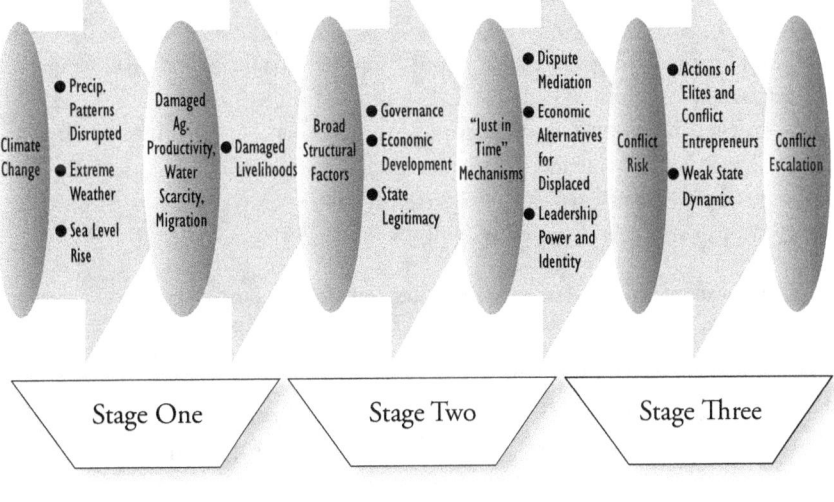

of the process and the factors in play. The purpose of the model is to move from the specifics of Darfur to a broader discussion of potential climate-related conflicts. The model draws on the themes associated with the escalation of the Darfur conflict, beginning with the impacts of climate change on livelihoods and the importance of governance and mediation, but it places these themes within a broader framework. The model (see Figure 14) draws on the insights of many authors, including the notable works of Julie Flint and Alex de Waal on Darfur, of Erik Nielsen (also on Darfur), of Barnett and Adger, and of Holsti; it arrives at some of the same conclusions as Homer-Dixon.[229] Buhaug, Gleditsch, and Theisen have proposed a model that shares some basic concepts with the one developed in this chapter.[230]

Figure 14 traces the process through which the physical impacts of climate change may potentially be transformed into conflicts. In this model, the effects of climate change, such as drought, may negatively affect the livelihoods of vulnerable groups through effects on agricultural productivity. This disruption of livelihoods can thrust different groups into competition and potential conflict. Whether such potential for conflict translates into conflict risk, however, depends crucially on several attributes of the society or state where the impacts of climate change are felt: governance, economic development, and state fragility or legitimacy. For purposes of this model, these attributes function as intervening variables, mediating the competition and potential for conflict. (Per MacKinnon, an intervening variable mediates or transmits the effect of an independent variable to a dependent variable.)[231] Each of these broad structural attributes of the state includes mechanisms that can be thought of as functioning in stages: some mediating competition long before tensions would emerge, and some that function as "just-in-time" mechanisms, mitigating and mediating emerging tensions and conflicts. Failure of these mechanisms can lead to situations with the potential for escalation to violence. Such escalation may be abetted by the actions of elites or conflict entrepreneurs and certain dynamics of weak states.

The following sections describe the potential process and provide examples.

Climate Change to Damaged Livelihoods

The first stage in the model above represents the process through which climate change affects livelihoods. In Darfur, long-term decrease in precipitation, combined with desertification and the extreme drought in 1982–1984, forced the Abbala Arab nomads of northern Darfur into sharp competition for water sources and land for grazing with the Fur, Masalit, and other farmers in central and southern Darfur. The climate changes in Darfur damaged the livelihoods of those vulnerable population groups and created a situation that was rife with the *potential* for conflict.

Future climate changes are likely to create similar circumstances, especially in weak states that depend on agriculture, by damaging livelihoods of vulnerable groups and thrusting them into competition. Disruption of existing precipitation patterns will lead to water scarcity and to greater competition over water sources among rural farmers and herders. Long-term droughts, such as those that led to migration in Darfur, will cause pressure for migration in other regions. Such migration can take place both domestically and internationally.

The underlying conflict in the case of Darfur was over water and land for grazing, as well as problems related to migration. In other cases, however, additional points of conflict may come into play. Some experts predict conflicts over water between rural groups and urban populations. Droughts that damage crops may lead to food scarcity and higher food prices, which can exacerbate distributional differences between different groups within states. Declining agricultural productivity due to nutrient runoff and topsoil erosion from increased incidence of flooding may damage rural incomes and increase pressure for groups to migrate. Sea level rise that undermines productivity and habitability of low-lying river deltas and small island states will pressure groups to migrate elsewhere, creating potential for competition and tensions with the migrants' new hosts.[232]

What is the evidence that such potential for climate-related conflicts may become a broader problem? In addition to specific cases such as that of Darfur, there is cross-sectional empirical work that reinforces the contention that climate shocks such as droughts can translate to increased conflict risk. Three studies—by Miguel et al., by Levy, and by Hendrix and Glazer—found that rainfall variations (i.e., drought) increase the risk of intrastate conflicts in subsequent years. The Miguel study and the Hendrix and Glazer study examined rainfall variation in Africa, where the high prevalence of rain-fed agriculture increases vulnerability to such variation, while Levy looked at rainfall variation on a global scale. The increased risk suggested by the Miguel study is comparatively large. When drought leads to a five-percent drop in income in the previous year (which is less than one standard deviation in per capita income growth), there is a twelve-percentage-point increase in the incidence of civil war. In their model, this represents an increase of nearly one-half in the average probability of conflict, although it is an increase from a low baseline risk.[233] The other two studies (the Levy study and the Hendrix and Glazer study) found similar effects of rainfall on conflict risk in subsequent years. As climate change is expected to increase the incidence of the sorts of climatic shocks these studies examined, the potential for conflicts would also be expected to increase.[234] The three empirical studies, however, do not settle the mechanism through which the increased risk occurs. This is what the model developed in this chapter, combined with the study of Darfur in the last, attempts to do.

Broad Structural Factors: Governance, Economic Development, and State Legitimacy

Situations with the potential for conflict are, of course, only the beginning of the story. Whether the competition and tensions that result from damaged livelihoods escalate into conflict depends critically on a state's strength of governance, level of economic development, and legitimacy. This is well established empirically, as the most repeated and robust findings in the quantitative studies on the causes of violent intrastate conflicts are the strong role that good governance and economic development have in lowering such risk.[235] It is also intuitive because dealing with competition and allocating scarce resources are among the most basic functions of political and economic institutions. In a parallel to governance and economic development, the legitimacy of the state affects its ability to address challenges requiring collective action, a point to which we will turn later.

In this model, good governance, economic development, and state legitimacy function as intervening variables between the *potential* for conflict created by climate change and the conflict risk itself. Governance, economic development, and state legitimacy may mitigate risk or exacerbate it, depending on their success. Many of the events related to themes of governance and politics/ideology that played a part in the escalation in Darfur, for example, would fall into the category of governance under this model.

For analytical purposes, the effects of governance, economic development, and state legitimacy can be split, as noted in Figure 15, into two sets, based on the timeframe in which they operate. The first set of attributes that function to mitigate conflict are broad structural factors, which function in the background and have longer-term impacts. A second set of effects include "just-in-time" mechanisms that function to mitigate conflict risk closer in time to the moment tensions emerge. We will turn to the just-in-time mechanisms below, but first will consider how the broad structural effects of governance, economic development, and state legitimacy affect the risk of conflict.

Governance: Technically capable and accountable systems of governance are robustly associated with lower levels of violent conflict, in quantitative studies.[236] There are multiple reasons for this finding, among them the effects of accountability on the leadership through elections and through a free media. In such situations, there are higher incentives for working out differences through the political process, rather than through violence. Moreover, the credibility of the political and judicial systems reinforces their ability to foster collective action to adapt to new challenges. Amartya Sen, the Nobel Prize–winning economist, found that, even in the face of acute environmental scarcities, countries with democratic institutions and press freedoms work to prevent famine precisely because democracies are accountable to their citizens.[237] Applied in the context of our climate change model, these findings suggest accountable governance will help ensure that states respond to their population's needs and act to lower vulnerability. The best of democratic intentions, however, may still be undermined by lack of institutional capacity. Miguel et al. found that relatively nondemocratic African countries hit by negative income shocks (i.e., droughts) are just as prone to civil conflict as relatively democratic countries, suggesting that even democratic states in Africa typically lack the institutional capability to adequately respond to negative economic shocks and avert conflict.[238]

How to define and measure governance, or institutional capacity, however, is not agreed upon in the academic literature. Studies use different proxies to measure institutional effectiveness, which, as noted, are robustly associated with lower conflict levels, but may be imperfect measures. We will use one such indicator, the United Nations Human Development

Index, as one variable in a vulnerability screen developed at the end of this chapter.

Economic Development: Despite repeated empirical findings that economic development is correlated with lower conflict risk, there is no general consensus in the economic literature on the mechanisms through which this occurs. Instead, the economic literature puts forward a number of potential explanations, all of which are intriguing but do not provide a systematic account. Collier et al. and Fearon and Laitin focused on how economic strength affects the related concepts of feasibility of rebellion and opportunity for rebellion, respectively.[239] Murshed and Tadjoeddin argue that, with higher income, people have more to lose from violence, while masses of impoverished individuals provide the best recruitment grounds for rebel fighters.[240] Works by Collier et al. and Gates single out the individual's calculation of his opportunity cost of rebelling as important factors in conflict risk.[241] Our model of climate change–related conflicts will put aside the still-evolving explanations by using the single concept of economic development.

One important aspect of how economic development affects the ultimate risk of conflict is the capacity of states to plan for adaptation to climate changes and invest in those plans, thereby reducing the vulnerability of their population to climate changes. Investments to develop water sources and irrigation schemes, for instance, can reduce vulnerability to changes in precipitation patterns. Such reduced vulnerability, in turn, will tend to diminish the negative impact of climate changes on livelihoods, thus lessening the potential for conflicts.[242] Conversely, states with low levels of economic development have limited capacity to plan and invest to reduce their vulnerability to climate shocks.

In Darfur, the British colonial authorities and the Sudanese state, in succession, did little to develop Darfur's infrastructure, including water infrastructure. This left the population of Darfur vulnerable to the climate changes the Sahel began to experience after 1971. The initial burden caused by this lack of investment was borne by Abbala camel-herding nomads of northern Darfur, who suffered most from climate changes and the 1982–1984 drought and famine; the Abbala saw 70 percent to 90 percent of their herds perish.[243] As explored in chapter three, these losses deepened their poverty and marginalization and contributed to the escalation of the Darfur conflict.[244]

Despite evidence in case studies and conflict prevention literature that poverty and inequality contributed to particular conflicts, the role of poverty and inequality is still debated in economic literature.[245] This is because aggregate measures of inequality have not been found to be significant correlates of conflict in quantitative cross-sectional studies; the aggregate data, however, suffer from limitations inasmuch as most measures of poverty and inequality are correlated with other economic and institutional weaknesses, leaving the precise causality unclear.[246] Nevertheless, detailed case studies of drought and its effects on income in Africa suggest that the impact of drought on income across economic classes is differentiated and that the real effect of drought may be to increase existing inequality.[247]

State Legitimacy: Holsti's 1996 analysis divides state legitimacy into two dimensions: vertical and horizontal. The vertical establishes "the connection ('the right to rule') between society and political institutions and regimes." The horizontal "defines the limits and criteria for membership in the political community which is ruled."[248] Strongly democratic and accountable governments are examples of strong vertical legitimacy. Horizontal legitimacy refers to how a citizen is defined. Examples of strong horizontal legitimacy include those states that define themselves and their citizens in terms of shared rights and responsibilities. A state that defines itself as the home of a particular ethnic or religious group will not enjoy broad horizontal legitimacy with other residents. The important point for purposes of the model of climate change–related conflicts is that states with legitimacy across different population groups are better able to forge collective solutions to climatic shocks. Conversely, in states without such legitimacy, the politics of identity are more likely to get in the way of collective responses, hindering the capacity—or the willingness—of the state to respond to those whose livelihoods have been affected by climate change.

In our case study of Darfur, we noted that the Sudanese state lacked legitimacy. This likely contributed to its militarized responses to the discontent and low-level violence in Darfur, since it perceived the unrest as a threat to its power. Instead of seeking political solutions, which would have required political buy-in from groups such as the Fur and Masalit, the Arab elite in Khartoum responded by arming tribal Arab proxies.

"Just-in-Time" Mechanisms: Dispute Mediation, Economic Alternatives, and Legitimacy

Now we turn to several attributes of governance, economic development, and state legitimacy that manifest themselves as just-in-time mechanisms, serving to mitigate and mediate emerging tensions and conflicts that may arise from climate change–related impacts on livelihoods.

Dispute Mediation: A technically capable and accountable government can mediate competition and conflicts among contending users of scarce resources, including environmental resources. Competent administrative authorities and judicial systems can help keep competition from escalating into broader conflict or even violence.

As we saw in the Darfur case study, the Sudanese government eliminated the tribal administration system in 1971, but Sudanese institutions did not fill the institutional void with regard to conflict mediation. The resulting lack of effective mediation of the disputes and low-level violence that occurred during and after the 1982–1984 drought allowed conflicts to fester. In some cases, where trust between groups remains high enough, tribal or clan mechanisms can be effective substitutes for state mediation to keep the peace. For example, Meier et al. document systemic low-level conflicts among different pastoral groups in the Horn of Africa. These do not break out into wider violence, in part because of traditional conflict mitigation mechanisms, including mediation by clan elders.[249] In a similar vein, Boege et al. argue that the semi-institutionalized role of tribal elders in Somaliland has helped Somaliland avoid much of the bloodshed that has plagued the rest of Somalia.[250] By contrast, Nyong worries that in the western Sahel, including far northern Nigeria, the effectiveness of traditional institutions as conflict mediators is being undermined:

> Local communities in the Sahel have developed systems to manage conflicts—including climate-related conflicts—that have been effective in the past. The apparent failure of these institutions to prevent the escalation of recent conflicts—such as those that have occurred in northern Nigeria; among the Turkana and the Maasai of Kenya; and among the Borona and Degodia in Ethiopia—can be attributed to the

juxtaposition of "modern" or "Western" tenure regimes with traditional regimes… rendering traditional conflict management strategies ineffective… and exacerbate the continuing loss of indigenous belief systems and practices.[251]

Economic Alternatives: For purposes of our model, in which population groups affected by climate change see their livelihoods disrupted, three aspects of economic development will likely be important for keeping conflict potential from escalating into conflict risk. These are

(1) The financial and logistical capacity of the local and regional authorities to provide temporary relief for those affected, be they ocal resident or displaced persons;

(2) Functioning markets that provide alternate means of meeting subsistence needs; and

(3) In cases where climate changes have permanent impacts on the livelihoods of certain population groups, states with strong economies are able to offer or develop alternate sources of livelihoods in other economic sectors. Weak economies offer fewer opportunities for farm households to diversify their sources of income with non-farm work, which is an important mechanism for coping with variable farm income.[252]

In the case of Darfur, lack of economic alternatives for those farmers and pastoralists who were affected by climate changes likely played a part in the escalation of the conflicts. The development strategy pursued by Khartoum concentrated what limited development resources it had on a few large-scale agriculture projects dedicated to export crops such as sugar or cotton, rather than on projects that would increase productivity in the traditional sectors.[253] The plantation projects earned valuable foreign exchange, but created relatively few jobs even as they displaced the small-holding farmers who had previously farmed the project lands.[254] Although a few Abbala Arabs migrated to the Persian Gulf to seek jobs in response to the climate changes and the 1982–1984 drought, the lack of economic alternatives in Darfur sharpened the effects of the drought on poverty. Moreover, Khartoum's administrative neglect of Darfur during the drought and famine likely contributed to the horrific toll in terms of mortality (an estimated 100,000 deaths) and un-resolved conflicts.[255] Better functioning and integration of markets during the famine could have helped Darfurians meet their food needs from other sources, but as Teklu notes, the very thin grain markets in Darfur led to a 500 percent increase in grain prices during that period, exacerbating the famine and its effects on poverty.[256]

Leadership Power and Identity: States that enjoy vertical and horizontal le-gitimacy foster trust among groups and between those groups and the gov-ernment, which allows for mediation of disputes and trust that economic de-velopment will be equitable. At this stage of the process, legitimacy serves as a reinforcing or complicating factor, affecting the effectiveness of governance and its efforts at conflict mediation. Carment argues that the lack of an im-partial arbiter, a role the state would normally play, exacerbates the problem of credible commitments in mediation.[257]

Where the state lacks horizontal legitimacy among its varied population groups, tensions and competition between population groups carry within them the latent potential to become identity conflicts, as many groups have not bought in to the same idea of the state.[258] Such a polarization along ethnic lines was one factor in the Darfur conflict. In addition, the govern-ment in fragile states often lacks a monopoly on violence, a fact that may increase the likelihood that groups will see violence as a feasible option to address their claims.

Applied to our model, to the extent that the state is unable to meet its re-sponsibilities to provide security and mediate conflicts, it creates a power vacuum that encourages groups adversely affected by climate change–related scarcity to take matters into their own hands as they seek to reestablish the security of their livelihoods. As Skaperdas notes, "The first step towards civil war is the creation of a power vacuum, of anarchy, whereby for a combina-tion of reasons the state effectively cedes control and physical and contrac-tual insecurity become rampant."[259] The neo-Malthusian theoretician Kahl noted in 2006 that groups left by the state to "fend for themselves" face such a security dilemma.[260]

Taking the idea of a security dilemma further, Posen and Lischer have applied the neorealist notion of the security dilemma in conflict between states to conflicts within the state. Lischer's framework includes political factors, such as oppressive government or a drive for hegemony over the state apparatus by one group, as causes of fear that may drive violence. In Lischer's analysis, war between factions or communal groups is triggered by "increased levels of fear and perceived feasibility of addressing threats using violence." In analyzing the concept of feasibility, Lischer stressed the concept of changes in perceptions or power balances, as indicated by "shifts in relative military capability, a weakened or distracted adversary, heightened public support, or international legitimacy and false optimism in one's chances of success."[261]

Conflict Risk

Although the effects of governance, economic development, and state legitimacy described above are undoubtedly important to conflict risk, they often shed little light on timing of conflicts or the particular dynamics through which the escalation from conflict potential to violence takes place. How escalation takes place in individual cases depends on the intricacies of individual states and regions, which vary significantly from case to case. Nevertheless, for purposes of our model of climate change–related conflicts, it is worth discussing in broad terms two particular factors—the actions of elites and conflict entrepreneurs, and the dynamics of weak states—that can abet the escalation of conflict potential to violence. The actions of individual leaders are often very difficult to predict, and the dynamics of weak states are sui generis, a point that underlines the importance of knowledgeable country and regional experts as the international community grapples with such potential conflicts.

Actions of Elites and Conflict Entrepreneurs in Forming Conflict Groups: One factor of conflict risk neglected by much of the environmental security literature is the actions of elites and conflict entrepreneurs. The term *elites* is used broadly here, to include influential economic and political groupings, as well as individual leaders. Such leaders face the complicated tasks of managing sometimes fractious states in the face of environmental, political, and economic stresses. While their choices may be constrained by structural factors, lack of institutional capability, and the support or opposition of other groups within the state, the decisions of elites are important to the ultimate risk of conflict, particularly in the early stages of crises. They also are a key interface for the international community.

For purposes of our model of potential climate-related conflicts, the most important issue is the occasional choice made by elites and societal leaders to take advantage of the tensions and competition that can result when livelihoods are disrupted to advance narrow interests in increasing their own power. Recent research on the role of individual agents in conflicts has examined the role of individuals termed variously *conflict entrepreneurs, ethnic entrepreneurs,* or *military entrepreneurs.* As Richard Jackson explains:

> What actually needs to be explained is how neighbors once ignorant of the very idea that they belonged to opposed civilizations begin to think—and hate—in these terms; how they vilify and demonize people they once called friends; how, in short, the seeds of mutual paranoia are sown, grain by grain, on the soil of a common life.... [C]onflict entrepreneurs attempt to deconstruct or discredit alternative discourses that oppose their own war aims—anti-war and anti-violence discourses, discourses of cultural inclusiveness, and moderate nationalist discourses. First, there is the well-known and well researched notion of identity formation. The creation of "the Other" as a constitutive outside the Self is a critical precondition to internal war.... It also necessary that groups stereotype, dehumanize, and scapegoat "the Other." This is part of what Bowman calls the "discursive project of transforming neighbors into enemies."[262]

The Darfur case study offers examples of the importance of the role of elites and conflict entrepreneurs. We noted the role of the "Committee of the Arab Gathering," a group of 23 prominent Darfurian Arabs who took advantage of the festering conflicts during and after the 1982–1984 drought and famine, as well as the increasing marginalization of Darfur's Abbala Arab population, to spread a radical and racist ideology. Individual tribal leaders, such as Janjawiid leader Musa Hilal, also played a role in fomenting conflict. The decisions by the Sudanese riverine Arab elite in Khartoum were obviously important as well, notably in arming proxies to deal with the discontent in Darfur instead of pursuing political solutions.[263]

A separate example of the role of elites and conflict entrepreneurs in fomenting conflict is the Rwanda genocide. The role of Hutu extremists, who methodically demonized the Tutsi and turned them into scapegoats for the country's problems, had President Habyarimana's aircraft shot down, and took advantage of the ensuing chaos to seize power and launch mass killings of the Tutsi, is well documented.[264] The conflict entrepreneurs' propaganda was all the more convincing for many Hutu because Rwanda faced very real demographic and environmental pressures, with insufficient arable land to support the burgeoning rural population and an economy that was not providing sufficient sources of non-farm employment.[265]

Climate change–related impacts on human livelihoods can enable the work of conflict entrepreneurs by creating intergroup competition and tensions that such entrepreneurs exploit to define a group, create a sense of victimization, and scapegoat others. Perceptions of a broken social contract and weakened state security institutions open up political space for conflict entrepreneurs to exploit. Carment argues that if the entrepreneurs' political and economic gains come disproportionately from the deprivation of rival groups, escalation toward conflict will be the result.[266]

Structural factors can facilitate or hinder the work of conflict entrepreneurs. In a democratic society, with a free press, accountability of elected officials, an educated populace, and sufficient economic opportunities, the discourse of conflict entrepreneurs will ring hollow for most. In states where there are large economic inequalities between groups or social classes, where the government is unelected and unaccountable, where institutions are unresponsive to the grievances of the population (whether for lack of capacity or willingness to help matters not in this case), and where people fear their livelihoods are vulnerable, conflict entrepreneurs will find much more fertile ground for their divisive, corrosive message. Weak states display many of the latter characteristics. Individual agency, however, is devilishly hard to predict or model.

Weak State Dynamics: In the case of fragile states, the impacts of climate change could change the dynamics of an intergroup struggle in ways that would trigger violent conflict when one group faces a security dilemma. One group's effort to secure its own livelihood is interpreted as a threat by other groups, which react in ways that are threatening to the first. Fear drives a cycle of escalation. A second way in which climate change might create the sort of fear that drives violence depends on the relative adaptability of the competing groups to climate change. This arguably was a factor in the Darfur conflict, where the way of life of the Bedouin Abbala camel herder groups was threatened when Fur farmers reacted to the drought and famine-driven camel herder incursions by beginning to fence off their fields and not allowing the herders passage or access to their water sources. Such fundamental changes could spark fear of cultural annihilation, which Lischer's framework posits could be expected to spark violence.[267] In the case of Darfur, the drought and famine did witness violence, which was initially isolated and localized. Critically, those conflicts were left festering by the failure of state and traditional tribal mediation mechanisms.

In such situations, fractionalization of society leads to identity-based politics, which exacerbate tensions. As Carment observes:

> As states begin to rely more extensively on coercive forms of managing internal (mostly ethnic) tensions, power tends to become more concentrated in the hands of a few and potentially homogenous groups. This disjuncture creates recurring problems of governability for those in power. The resulting breakdown begins at the state center as hierarchical patterns of authority give way to regional, decentralized, ethnic, and informal forms of political and economic organization.[268]

Migration: A Wildcard

For purposes of the basic model in this chapter, migration is viewed as having effects on livelihoods similar in some ways to environmental impacts. Like the direct effects of climate changes, flows of migrants may increase competition over scarce environmental resources. The competition and conflict potential that their arrival creates in host societies or regions are mediated by the institutional framework (governance, economic development, and legitimacy) of that state or region. They differ from direct environmental effects in two key ways. First, since they often move great distances, migrants can transmit the effects of local or regional climatic shocks across international borders, and even across continents. Second, given their nature as outsiders, migrants represent particularly inviting targets for conflict entrepreneurs, be they politicians or warlords, who seek to use them to stoke identity-based passions.[269]

It is well established that environmental factors have long played a part in decisions to migrate. Case studies of the "dust bowl" drought on the Great Plains of the United States in the 1930s have documented the role that long-term drought, soil erosion, and falling agricultural productivity played in the migration of millions to other parts of the United States. Separately, land scarcity, land degradation, and flooding have led up to 17 million Bangladeshis to migrate to the neighboring states of Assam and Tripura, India, since the 1950s. The ultimate decision to migrate, of course, will always be multifaceted, with factors such as poverty and lack of alternate economic opportunities in the home region playing a large role as well. Moreover, migration can be both a cause and a result of environmental changes.[270]

Waves of migration can lead to violence under certain conditions. Many migrants fleeing the dust-bowl drought headed to California, where they competed with natives for jobs, land, and other resources. It has been documented how natives beat the migrants, burned their shacks, and accused them of being communists; Los Angeles police at one point were sent to the California border to try to keep the migrants out.[271] In the Indian states of Assam and Tripura, competition, primarily over agricultural land, led to violent clashes in the early 1980s; during a five-hour 1983 rampage, an estimated 1,700 migrant Bengalis from Bangladesh were killed in Assam.[272] Tensions between migrants and hosts over internal migration within Bangladesh were a factor in the insurgency of the 1980s and 1990s.[273]

Two aspects of the Darfur case study illustrate how migration can contribute to conflicts. We saw how climate changes starting in the early 1970s, combined with severe drought and famine in 1982–1984, forced the Arab Abbala nomads of northern Darfur to migrate to find water and pasture for their livestock, thrusting them into competition and occasionally violent conflict with farmers.[274] Then, as tensions continued to rise in Darfur due to Khartoum's administrative neglect of the drought and famine, Chadian Arab refugees, fleeing Chad after the overthrow of Habré, began migrating to Darfur. These refugees exacerbated environmental pressures in many areas; many fought with their Darfurian Arab "kin" against the Fur in the first Arab-Fur war, from 1987–1989.[275]

Although violence is possible when migrants move, that result is not a given, even where they compete with existing residents over land and resources.

Half (19 of the 38 cases) of the environmentally influenced migrations that Reuveny documents, some with migrant flows numbering in the millions, did not lead to violence.[276] The works of Goldstone, as well as Teitelbaum and Winter, suggest that the political and institutional response to an influx of new migrants is the key factor in determining whether flows of immigration spark conflict. Teitelbaum and Winter find that the main potential for conflict results when migration leads to a clash of identities.[277] Identity itself can be a malleable concept, however, as many new states have forged new national identities where before there were many, or none.[278]

Another significant expected source of pressure for migration is sea-level rise, which in this century may begin to affect the livelihoods of as many as 56 million people in low-lying regions worldwide, including the Nile delta and the Mekong River delta in Vietnam. Roughly nine percent of Egypt's population of 78.8 million live within one meter of sea level. Eleven percent of Vietnam's population of 88.6 million live within one meter of sea level, while the low-lying Mekong delta region represents half of the country's rice production. Eight percent of Mauritania's population and seven percent of Suriname's population are similarly exposed. Roughly 1.1 percent of Bangladesh's population of 156.1 million live within one meter of sea level, notably in the low-lying Ganges-Brahmaputra delta. In the face of threatened livelihoods due to inundations of the lowest-lying regions, erosion of productive land, and salt-water intrusion into aquifers, some portion of this population will choose to abandon their homes, creating substantial numbers of new migrants. Sea level rise will also constitute an economic shock in many of these vulnerable countries.[279]

Even large-scale migration need not lead to violence, but refugee movements can have destabilizing effects on the social and political balance within states. Climate change has the potential to create millions of new migrants, resulting in significant pressures on institutional capacity, particularly in developing economies. The risk of violent anti-migrant backlash is considerable.[280]

It is worth noting that environmental migrants can become political factors in unexpected ways. Drought induced the emigration of Tuareg in the 1970s and 1980s from northern Mali, Malawi, and Nigeria to Algeria and Libya, which led to many of them being exposed to radical Islamic ideas. Upon their return, many of these Tuareg became involved in a low-level rebellion.[281]

Internal conflicts in Rwanda and Burundi led to the migration of Hutu and Tutsi groups to the Democratic Republic of the Congo, which contributed to destabilizing ethnic wars in the eastern portion of that country.[282] In both cases, migration transmitted destabilizing political effects across international boundaries.

Finally, while environmental migrants may be driven to move great distances, in most cases, environmentally driven migration takes place within countries or regions. This will make the problem of climate change–driven migration more likely to be one of internally displaced persons and refugees from within the region, rather than intercontinental migration.[283]

Vulnerability Screen

This section develops a rough vulnerability screen, which represents an attempt to identify those states that are the most vulnerable to climate change–related conflicts as suggested by the model developed in this chapter.[284] To do so, it combines proxy measurements of physical vulnerability to climate change with measures of strength of governance, economic development, and state legitimacy. Figure 15 relates the variables chosen to the stages in the model developed in Figure 14. The physical effects of climate change, from the first two stages of our model, are together represented as the first stage in the screen below. The structural factors explored in the model (governance, economic development, and state legitimacy; the third and fourth stages of the model) are represented in the middle blue box in Figure 15. The last

Figure 15: Vulnerability Screen

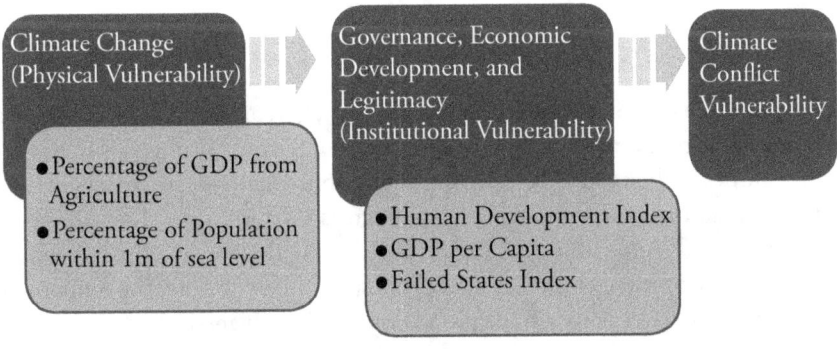

stages of the model, relating to conflict escalation, do not lend themselves to this simple vulnerability screening exercise, and are thus not represented. This screen draws on work by Barnett and Adger, as well as by Schwartz.[285]

The Variables: This screen uses two indicators to represent physical vulnerability to climate changes. First, it uses the percentage of Gross Domestic Product (GDP) produced by the agricultural sector as a rough measure of vulnerability of livelihoods to climatic fluctuations. This measure is inspired by several studies, including by Hendrix and Glazer, Miguel et al., and Levy, finding that droughts increase conflict risk in subsequent years.[286] It also draws on the results of the case study of Darfur, where we saw vulnerability to climatic fluctuations was high because of the region's high dependence on rain-fed agriculture, both farming and pastoral, which represented over 80 percent of the Darfur's employment in the 1980s.[287] The second indicator of physical vulnerability to climate change used here is the percentage of the population that lives within one meter of sea level, which would correlate with a state's vulnerability to sea level rise.[288]

To screen for institutional vulnerability, which our model and the Darfur case study suggest are important factors in climate-conflict vulnerability, we use three proxies for the structural factors (including their "just-in-time" mechanisms) identified: governance, economic development, and state legitimacy. Following on several of the empirical studies on intrastate conflict risk, this screen uses the United Nations Human Development Index (HDI) as a proxy for strength or weakness of governance. To proxy state legitimacy, the screen uses the Fund for Peace/Foreign Policy Magazine Failed States Index. The Failed States Index is a composite index composed of expert assessments of twelve different measures of state fragility.[289]

Discussion of Screening Results

The full results of the screen are reported in the chart at the end of this chapter. The chart lists the twenty-four worst scoring countries in each of these five measures of vulnerability. Given the limitations of the data used here, and the basic nature of our model, the risk factors in this screen should be considered broad vulnerabilities, rather than predictions that climate change will lead any of these countries into conflict.[290] Nevertheless, the vulnerability of several states across multiple measures of both institutional weakness and physical vulnerability to climate change merits special mention. These states are Afghanistan, Burkina Faso, Central African Republic, Chad, Cote d'Ivoire, Democratic Republic of the Congo, Ethiopia, Eritrea, Liberia, Mali, Mozambique, Sudan, and Uganda. These 13 countries combine institutional weaknesses with a high economic dependence on agriculture, most of which is rain fed, leaving them more vulnerable than others to the expected increase in the variability of precipitation patterns. On an encouraging note, none of the states that are the most exposed to sea-level rise ranks among the very weakest in terms of governance, economic development, or state fragility. Nevertheless, the sheer number of persons vulnerable to a one-meter sea-level rise in Vietnam and Egypt makes those two countries worth watching.[291]

Conclusion

The path from the physical impacts of climate change to violent intrastate conflict explored in this chapter is neither a direct one nor, thankfully, a given one. While climate change is very likely to disrupt livelihoods, create environmental refugees, and exacerbate competition over scarce environmental resources, notably water, resolving this sort of competition and mediating conflicts is part of the normal course of business for the political, social, and economic institutions of a healthy state. In fragile states with low institutional capacity and characterized by a lack of legitimacy, such conflicts may remain unmediated and worsen. Low levels of economic development will tend to keep such states from making investments that will reduce the vulnerability of their populations and will keep those whose livelihoods have been affected by climate change from building new livelihoods or finding alternate sources of income. In such cases, there is the potential for the conflicts and increased competition caused by climate change's impacts on livelihoods to escalate and turn violent, as they did in Darfur. This depends as well on the actions of individual leaders and group elites, as they grapple with the security dilemma facing them in the absence of an effective state and institutional response. In addition, such situations are ripe for the depredations of conflict entrepreneurs. The good news is that the pathways from climate change to conflict identified herein contain several points at which the international community can engage using the tools of economic and institutional development policy, as well as of preventive diplomacy, to avert or mitigate such conflicts. This is the subject to which we will turn in the last chapter.

Chart—Structural and Environmental Vulnerability Related Indices									
Vulnerability to Sea Level Rise		Vulnerability to Rainfall Variation		Governance		Economic Development		State Fragility or Legitimacy	
Country name	% Population within 1m of Sea Level	Country name	2011 Agriculture, value added (% of GDP)	Country name	2011 Human Development Index Rank	Country name	2010 GDP Per Capita, $PPP	Country name	2011 Failed State Index
Myanmar	1.10	Kyrgyz Republic	20	Zambia	164	East Timor	1439	Syria	154
Morocco	1.50	Tajikistan	20	Djibouti	165	Tanzania	1435	Eritrea	155
Qatar	1.80	Albania	20	Rwanda	166	Uganda	1275	North Korea	156
China (PRC)	2	Armenia	21	Benin	167	Burkina Faso	1261	Myanmar	157
Liberia	2	Zambia	21	Gambia	168	Afghanistan	1202	Uganda	158
Senegal	2	Nicaragua	21	Sudan	169	Nepal	1198	Niger	159
Belize	2	Pakistan	22	Côte d'Ivoire	170	Guinea-Bissau	1181	Burundi	160
Saudi Arabia	2	Paraguay	22	Malawi	171	Rwanda	1155	Ethiopia	161
Libya	3	Kenya	23	Afghanistan	172	Haiti	1101	Kenya	162
Djibouti	3	Uganda	23	Zimbwe	173	Comoros	1092	Guinea-Bissau	163
Taiwan	3	Côte d'Ivoire	24	Ethiopia	174	Guinea	1086	Nigeria	164
Puerto Rico	3	Tanzania	27	Mali	175	Mali	1073	Pakistan	165
Uruguay	3	Sudan	27	Guinea-Bissau	176	Ethiopia	1035	Guinea	166
The Gambia	4	The Gambia	30	Guinea	178	Madagascar	964	Central African Republic	168
Bahamas	4.20	Lao PDR	31	Central African Republic	179	Mozambique	913	Iraq	169

Chart—Structural and Environmental Vulnerability Related Indices, cont.									
Vulnerability to Sea Level Rise		**Vulnerability to Rainfall Variation**		**Governance**		**Economic Development**		**State Fragility or Legitimacy**	
Country name	% Popu-lation within 1m of Sea Level	Country name	2011 Agri-culture, value added (% of GDP)	Country name	2011 Human Develop-ment Index Rank	Country name	2010 GDP Per Capita, $PPP	Country name	2011 Failed State Index
Tunisia	4.50	Mozam-bique	32	Sierra Leone	180	Malawi	883	Yemen	170
UAE	4.50	Burundi	35	Burkina Faso	181	Sierra Leone	823	Haiti	171
French Guiana	6	Papua New Guinea	36	Liberia	182	Central African Republic	785	Afghani-stan	172
Guyana	6.50	Nepal	38	Chad	183	Niger	772	Zimbab-we	173
Suri-name	7	Guatemala	41	Mozam-bique	184	Burundi	581	Chad	174
Mauri-tania	8	Ethiopia	42	Burundi	185	Eritrea	543	Sudan	175
Egypt	9	Togo	43	Niger	186	Liberia	535	Congo (DROC)	176
Vietnam	11	Sierra Leone	44	Congo (DROC)	187	Congo (DROC)	351	Somalia	177

Data Sources: UNDP, World Bank, Dasgupta (2007), and *Foreign Policy* Magazine

Notes on the data:

The Human Development index is calculated by the U.N. Development Program, and is derived from measures of health, education, and standard of living.[292]

Data on per capita Gross Domestic Product (GDP) and on the percentage of GDP from agriculture were taken from the World Bank's online statistical database.[293]

The Failed States Index is produced by the Fund for Peace and by *Foreign Policy* magazine, and is based on expert assessments of twelve variables that contribute to state vulnerability. These are Demographic Pressures, Refugees/IDPs, Group Grievance, Human Flight, Uneven Development, Economic Decline, De-legitimatization of the State, Public Services, Human Rights, Security Apparatus, Factionalized Elites, and External Intervention.[294]

The data on population within one meter of sea level are taken from Dasgupta.[295]

Chapter Five

Preventing and Mitigating Climate Change–Related Conflicts

Overview

Intermediate-scale climate changes, as we have seen in the previous chapters, are likely to increase the *potential* for conflicts as populations adjust to changes in the environmental systems that support their livelihoods. This potential for conflict results when climate changes upset existing arrangements for the sharing of resources such as water and agricultural land. The mechanisms through which this occurs may be due to the direct effects of climate changes, such as droughts, flooding, sea-level rise, and long-term degradation of agricultural lands, or indirect effects, such as the displacement of population groups, which can then upset previous political and economic balances in the receiving regions.

> "Armed conflicts are increasingly concentrated in the poorest and most vulnerable portion of the world's countries. Future environmental changes will place further strains on these countries, possibly reducing the prospects for conflict resolution and sustained economic growth." —Buhaug et al., *Implications of Climate Change for Armed Conflict* (2008)

Governing such competition and solving disputes between rival users of resources is one of the fundamental functions of economic and sociopolitical systems. States that have legitimacy across population groups, strong courts, developed institutional planning mechanisms, and strong economies are very likely to be able to manage the effects of climate change before they take on a dynamic with a potential for violence. The well-developed international architecture for managing interstate disputes, including the web of treaties and arrangements governing transboundary waters, plays a similar role at the interstate level.

The potential for violent conflict nevertheless remains within those weak or fragile states whose institutions, economy, and sociopolitical systems are unable to manage the impacts of climate change on their populations. Chapter Three explored how climate change thrust groups into competition over land and water in Darfur, and how the conflict escalated because of failures in governance and the formation of conflict groups. Chapter Four placed the process that took place in Darfur into a broader model of the process through which climate change might lead to conflicts and what factors might be vulnerabilities. This final chapter will analyze the problem of preventing and mitigating climate change–related conflicts, in view of the risk factors and dynamics already identified.

Although the empirical literature on environmental security does not clearly establish the extent to which climate change–related conflicts are a risk, there are sound reasons to remain watchful.

- First, climate change will exacerbate the sort of climatic extremes, such as acute drought, that have contributed to conflict in cases such as Darfur.

- Second, the challenges of security, development, and governance in fragile and failing states are interrelated. To the extent that climate change exacerbates those challenges, these states may pose heightened risks for regional and international security.

- Third, conflict prevention using diplomatic and development policy tools will invariably be cheaper, in both human and monetary terms, than dealing with disaster later.[296]

To inform our exploration of ways in which climate change–related conflicts might be prevented, this chapter first briefly outlines a couple of relevant findings in the growing literature on conflict prevention and preventive diplomacy and discusses the cost-effectiveness of conflict prevention. The chapter then returns to the model developed in the last chapter to help visualize how conflict prevention might be accomplished in the context of climate change–related conflicts. It discusses some of the challenges of conflict prevention in the fragile state context and concludes with recommendations for those elaborating climate change–related conflict prevention strategies.

Methods of Conflict Prevention and Preventive Diplomacy

How then to prevent or mitigate the potential for climate change–related conflicts? Two main schools of thought exist, as expressed in recent conflict prevention and preventive diplomacy literature—a literature that has grown substantially since the 1990s. These schools emphasize operational conflict prevention and structural conflict prevention, respectively.

(1) Operational Conflict Prevention

This school of thought focuses primarily on methods and measures to mitigate tensions that are growing toward a crisis. Operational conflict prevention methods are meant to be employed close in time to the potential crisis point. Operational prevention includes "measures such as fact-finding and monitoring missions, negotiation, mediation, the creation of channels for dialogue among contending groups, preventive deployments, and confidence-building measures."[297] Neutral outside parties, such as the United Nations or regional multilateral organizations, are well placed to mitigate tensions using such methods, but these can also be implemented by local authorities, national authorities, or community leaders. Operational prevention is typically reactive, and represents a response triggered by the emergence of tensions.[298]

(2) Structural Prevention

While not dismissing the value and necessity of operational prevention, a second school of thought focuses greater attention on what they call "structural" conflict prevention. Structural conflict prevention serves to prevent conflicts by addressing the underlying roots of conflicts through "measures that facilitate governance, adherence to human rights, and economic, political, and societal stability, as well as civil society building."[299] Such structural measures are proactive and long-term in nature, and seek to create a framework in which conflicts are mediated well before they reach a crisis point, for instance by strengthening institutions or the rule of law. There is agreement in the conflict prevention literature that, to be effective, conflict prevention must be context-specific (i.e., designed for a specific country or region) and institutionalized, not only in states, but also among the international community. Ackerman singles out the Organization for Security and Cooperation in Europe (OSCE) as a positive example among multilateral organizations of institutionalizing conflict prevention measures.[300]

Utility of Conflict Prevention

Why bother with conflict prevention? Certainly, there is a natural humanitarian instinct to prevent violence and its toll in human suffering and death, but pragmatic national interests are also at stake. Conflicts, even entirely domestic ones, impose costs and have security impacts that are felt well beyond the conflicted state or region. The work of the state failure task force, which found that the presence of civil conflicts in bordering states was a strong predictor of state failure, reinforces this point.[301] Such an effect on neighbors may be transmitted through refugee flows or through economic costs in terms of lost trade. Refugees associated with Chadian civil war, for example, had a perverse impact in Darfur, while those fleeing the Rwandan genocide contributed to chaos in the Democratic Republic of the Congo.[302] Domestic conflicts can draw in neighbors, as occurred with the multiple interventions by neighbors in the Democratic Republic of the Congo or, in some cases, in West Africa. Just as problematically, the chaos of conflict can create ungoverned spaces, in which transnational networks—be they terrorist, criminal, or both—can find safe haven. The calculation that regional conflicts and ungoverned spaces pose a danger to U.S. security interests is reflected in the last three U.S. National Security Strategy documents, which call for efforts to prevent regional conflicts and address the problem of fragile and failing states and ungoverned spaces, in concert with U.S. allies.[303] As François and Sud point out, conflict prevention is "a public good warranting global cooperation and action."[304]

In practical terms, conflict prevention is also significantly cheaper than military intervention during a conflict, peacekeeping operations, or reconstruction after a conflict. Chalmers examined the costs and benefits of conflict prevention in six case studies and found that conflict prevention is highly cost effective, even when the assessment is based exclusively on financial costs and savings that accrue to the international community. On average across the scenarios examined, successful conflict prevention resulted in a 4:1 savings ratio for the international community over the costs of intervention and peacekeeping. A broader accounting of the savings of conflict prevention would result in a more positive ratio, because it would include the savings in terms of prevention of damages to infrastructure, saving human lives, and reducing or preventing the costs of a conflict to its neighbors (refugee flows, lost trade, etc.).[305]

Finally, there are political and budgetary limits on the capacity of the international community to intervene militarily in conflicts. An emphasis on prevention may be the most realistic option for the international community to deal with the potential for climate change–related conflicts, particularly in a time of stressed budgets. Expenditures on activities that have conflict prevention effects should be prioritized as investments in reducing the financial burden of crisis intervention later.[306]

Applying Conflict Prevention to Climate Change–Related Conflicts

Returning to the model of climate change–related conflict developed in the previous chapter (see, also, Figure 16), each of the stages in the trajectory from the physical effects of climate changes to conflicts offers opportunities for governments, local communities, and the international community to apply the tools of conflict prevention outlined above to reduce the potential for conflict. Measures to halt the potential progression from climate change

Figure 16: Model of Steps from Climate Change to Conflict

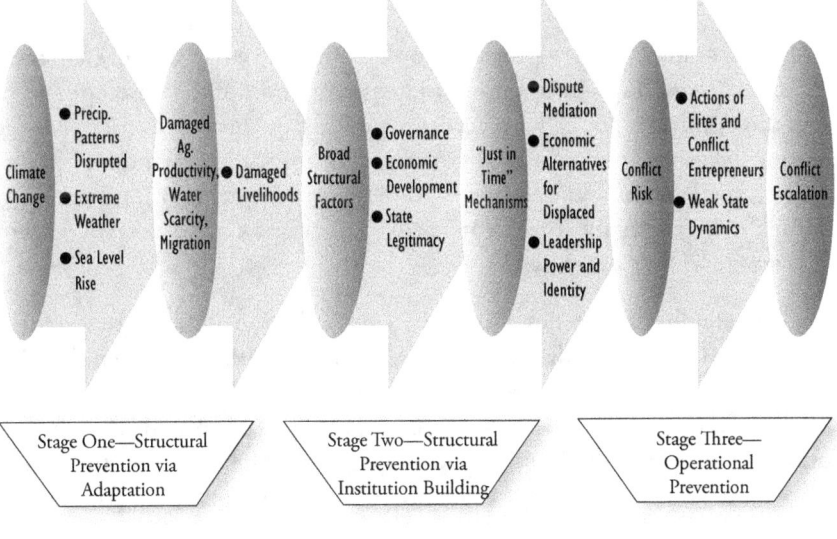

to conflict, when applied in first two stages of this model, would be analogous to structural conflict prevention methods identified in the conflict prevention literature. Efforts to mitigate climate change–related conflicts in the last stage of their progression can be compared to the operational prevention concept of that literature. The following sections examine each of these stages in greater detail and highlight the types of conflict prevention measures that may be effective at each.

Structural Conflict Prevention through Adaptation

In the first stage of the model, first-order effects of climate change, such as precipitation disruptions and declining productivity in agriculture, may damage livelihoods and force vulnerable population groups into competition over environmental resources. Much like the structural prevention measures examined in the conflict prevention literature, actions that reduce vulnerability to climate change by increasing adaptability would also play a conflict prevention role. Governments, local communities, and the international community could begin conflict prevention efforts by reducing vulnerability to climate changes. Examples include investments to improve agricultural productivity or to build water infrastructure such as wells, dams, and irrigation schemes. Increased availability of these environmental resources will reduce the potential for, or degree of, inter-group competition, as long as availability is accompanied by broad access.

To be most effective, such projects should be implemented as proactive measures, before tensions occur, rather than as a reaction to the development of tensions. Priority should be placed on projects in those countries that are most vulnerable to climate change–related conflicts. The mantra of prioritization by risk should also apply within countries, giving priority to those populations and regions that are particularly exposed to climatic variations or that have a history of tensions.

The vulnerability screen developed in Chapter Four highlighted the particular exposure of certain African countries to rainfall variations, given the high percentage of their GDP derived from agriculture and their dependence on rainfall. Water-supply experts stress the importance of groundwater for improving rural water supply and argue for greater research on water storage and its potential role in relieving water scarcity.[307] Greater provision will need to be made for water catchment and storage, irrigation projects, and greater use of groundwater sources (wells) to reduce the vulnerability of the populations of these states to climate changes. The effectiveness of such projects will be greater if planners keep the issue of broad access to water at the forefront.[308]

The IPCC suggests using the process of planning for water projects as an opportunity to forge peaceful cooperation between societal groups. Support for stakeholder dialogue and improving customary and formal governance (e.g., helping to allocate water or land rights, resolve disputes, and ensure equitable compensation) can serve as a confidence-building mechanism. Moreover, stakeholder involvement is crucial to risk, adaptation, and vulnerability assessments because it is the stakeholders who will be most affected by climate change and will need to find ways to adapt. In addition, this sort of stakeholder dialogue is important not only to acceptance of the project in question, but also to building networks between communities. Such networks increase knowledge about how to adapt to climate changes and can later aid in communication and mediation when conflicts do arise.[309]

Figure 17: Stages of Preventive Action

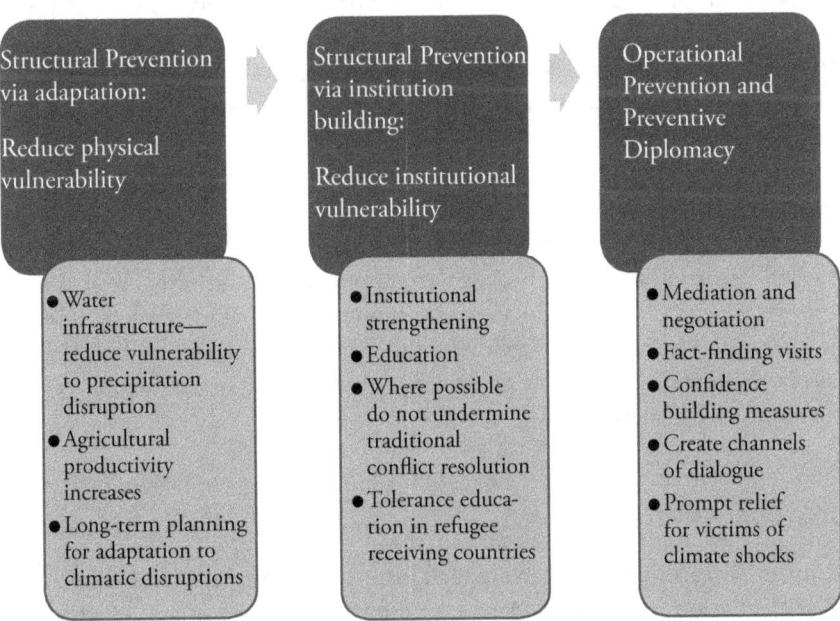

Although problems of water scarcity are likely to proliferate in the future, flooding events may ultimately affect a larger number of people and cause greater economic losses than drought. Using historical data since 1960 from the Center for Research in Epidemiology of Disaster, Blankenspoor et al.: "The risk of loss [from flooding] has increased significantly, and the population subject to risk has more than doubled. Droughts present a very different case, dominated by catastrophic events in a few countries...."[310] Apart from the direct damage caused by the catastrophic event, flooding and more concentrated rainfall can affect agricultural productivity by washing away nutrients in the soil.[311]

In addition to water-related projects, a second set of investments that could decrease climate-change vulnerability are those directed at improving agricultural productivity. Such investments would better position the extensive rural agricultural sectors in vulnerable states to withstand climatic variation, thereby decreasing the potential for tensions. The priority should be the development of seed strains that are tolerant of precipitation extremes—both dry and wet. Maintaining and even improving agricultural productivity in the face of greater climatic variation will protect rural livelihoods.

A good example of the sorts of agricultural productivity investments that will be necessary in developing countries is the work of the Brazilian Agricultural Research Corporation (EMBRAPA, its Portuguese acronym), which has increased agricultural yields in Brazil through the elaboration of new strands of food crops adapted to Brazil's highly varied climatic regions. This kind of investment will be necessary, particularly to create seed stocks tolerant of wide variations in precipitation. In a 2009 report, the International Food Policy Research Institute called for investments of roughly $7.3 billion to increase agricultural productivity sufficiently to offset the negative impacts of climate change on agricultural productivity; without such efforts, they predict declining calorie consumption by children in developing countries.[312] How best to assess vulnerability to climate change, and thereby how best to adapt, remains an evolving endeavor.

Structural Climate Change–Related Conflict Prevention through Institution Building

During the second stage of the model, institutional responses, including conflict mediation and provision of economic alternatives, may help mediate and mitigate tensions and competition when livelihoods are disrupted by climate change. Given the evidence that institutional strength reduces conflict risk, enhancing the strength of institutions in vulnerable states should have conflict-prevention effects. This strategy is analogous to the institutional strengthening called for by the structural conflict prevention literature, and includes strengthening rule of law, economic stability, and the technical capacity of institutions.

Strong local institutions are indispensable in conflict prevention due to their role in mediating competition and disputes among the population. Strong local institutions are also vital to analyzing local vulnerabilities to climate fluctuations and planning for their mitigation. In addition, strong institutions may help reduce the political space for conflict entrepreneurs to take advantage of tensions to build their conflict narratives.

Examples of effective institution-building policies could include investment in female education. Recent research by the Center for Global Development suggests that female education can be a cost-effective way to increase adaptability to extreme weather events in poor countries.[313] Women's education will help improve their capacity to deal with increased climate variability, which will be important in many lesser-developed countries where women disproportionately are the primary laborers on family subsistence farms.[314]

Strong institutions would also help deal with the potential for conflicts that result from the migration of population groups into new regions due to environmental pressures. Such movements, as we have seen, can put newcomers in competition with the existing residents of the area for basic resources such as land, water, and livelihoods (e.g., jobs, farms). Conflict, let alone violence, is not preordained in such cases. The reaction of local leaders and institutions to the migrant influx, however, is important to ensuring that relations among groups remain amicable and prevent conflict entrepreneurs from taking advantage of the inevitable tensions. In addition, investments in tolerance education in migrant-receiving countries will help prepare for these situations.

While institution building is seen as important to reducing climate conflict risk, it is less clear how to build institutional strength, especially in fragile states. It is a complex problem, some aspects of which will be discussed below.

Operational Prevention of Climate Change–Related Conflicts

Should conflicts remain unaddressed, they may reach the final stage of the model, where conflict entrepreneurs take advantage of tensions for their own power-seeking ends and the response of elites may help fan, or douse, the emerging flames. In such cases, national, regional, and local governments, when appropriate with the support of the international community, may use the well-known tools of operational conflict prevention and preventive diplomacy. These include mediation, fact-finding visits by outside parties, confidence-building measures, and international engagement with leaders and elites.[315] International engagement in such cases may be carried out through the United Nations; regional or subregional organizations, such as the African Union; the Organization for Security and Cooperation in Europe (OSCE); or by partnering with national, regional, local, or tribal political leadership, as appropriate. Multilateral leadership of international conflict mitigation efforts will often be preferred over bilateral ones. This is because bilateral actors are less likely to be seen as impartial, as states have interests that may be affected by the outcome of the conflict. Multilateral conflict prevention efforts, however, must be closely coordinated with the international community to be effective, as states are the ultimate source of the resources necessary to support conflict prevention. In other cases, states may be better positioned to lead such efforts, due to questions of political and economic influence to support conflict prevention. Flexibility and creativity in international efforts will be paramount.

Operational conflict prevention in climate change–related conflicts will also need to include relief efforts to meet the immediate needs of affected populations, including migrants and refugees fleeing war or climate disasters. To the extent that such needs are met, the scope for tension and conflict is reduced. Relief efforts, ideally locally led with international support, may help stop the cycle of migration before it starts. Helping victims of climatic shocks to build new livelihoods will also likely prevent tension and conflict.

One area where the international community will need to be assertive is in confronting the racist and xenophobic discourse of conflict entrepreneurs. Allowing this discourse to stand unchallenged contributes to the cycle of fear and violence. When local leaders and elites do not denounce such discourse, the international community should be prepared to use behind-the-scenes diplomacy to obtain such condemnation from local leaders. Should quiet diplomacy fail, the international community must be prepared publicly to denounce and expose the conflict discourse. Such international involvement in domestic politics can be thorny. Under most circumstances, it will be more effective if the message comes from regional or multilateral organizations, but it can be reinforced with coordinated messages, both public and private, by bilateral actors as well. Direct contacts behind the scenes with the conflict entrepreneur should also be attempted, with remonstrations about their corrosive public discourse combined with offers to investigate grievances and facilitate communication.

The simplicity of the above outline of conflict prevention for the stages of climate-related conflicts should not be read as suggesting that the challenges of implementing them will be small. We turn to some of those challenges next.

The Fragile State Context and Challenges to Preventing Climate Change–Related Conflicts

There is a growing recognition in the development community that, at least in the fragile state context, the problems of governance, economic development, and security are inextricably intertwined. As World Bank President Robert Zoellick argues:

> The trauma of fragile states and the interconnections of globalization require our generation to recognize anew the nexus among economics, governance and security....This is about securing development—bringing security and development together, first to smooth the transition from conflict to peace, and then to embed stability, so that development can take hold over a decade and beyond....Fragility and poverty alone do not necessarily lead to conflict, but low and stagnant incomes, unemployment, and ineffective government can create an environment that sparks violence.[316]

One of the basic conclusions of this study is that those states most vulnerable to climate conflicts are fragile states where institutional weakness and lack of economic development will hinder efforts to reduce vulnerability or to mediate conflicts when these do arise. Fragile and failing states are already in the international policy spotlight, as the security risks of "ungoverned spaces" associated with some of these states have been laid bare by their use as safe havens by terrorist networks, criminal networks, or both. Climate change–related conflicts could exacerbate this problem.

The international community will face two major challenges and one lesser challenge as it grapples with the question of structural conflict prevention for climate change–related conflicts. These are

(1) The unintended consequences of previous decisions on the prioritization of aid spending;

(2) The difficulty inherent in development spending and institution building in the fragile-state context; and

(3) The need to incorporate diverse actors in states with hybrid political orders.

Prioritization of Assistance

There has been a considered and entirely justifiable emphasis since the late 1990s for donors to give priority in the allocation of development assistance to those countries pursuing a comprehensive agenda of policy reforms or meeting certain benchmarks for institutional performance. This rational policy decision was meant to maximize the effectiveness of assistance dollars in terms of poverty reduction and growth. The move grew out of research findings, including prominent works by Burnside and Dollar, which found that such aid has the largest effect on growth, and thereby on poverty reduction, in those countries pursuing particular policy frameworks.[317] These findings understandably have led donors to try to maximize the growth impact of their limited assistance dollars by prioritizing aid to certain countries.[318] That same desire to maximize aid effectiveness led the U.S. government to create the Millennium Challenge Account in 2004, which focuses its assistance activities in countries that meet certain benchmarks of institutional performance.[319]

Aid Orphans

The rational policy choice of aid prioritization had the unintended side effect of creating what some have described as "aid orphans": states with fragile institutions, fragile economies, and few friends.[320] Using data from the Organization for Economic Cooperation and Development's Donor Advisory Committee (OECD-DAC), Levin and Dollar conclude that, as a group, states with weak institutions and policies received 43 percent less aid than their level of poverty, their population, and policy/institutional performance would predict. Within this group, post-conflict countries, such as Afghanistan, received much more aid than predicted by their level of poverty, population, and policy/institutional framework, while several "aid orphans" received much less aid than predicted by these variables. The aid orphans Levin and Dollar identify are Burundi, Central African Republic, Democratic Republic of the Congo, Republic of the Congo, Niger, Nigeria, Sudan, Togo, and Uzbekistan.[321] In the case of U.S. assistance flows, a separate 2006 Center for Global Development study by Patrick and Brown examined the 2007 U.S. budget request. They note that, while the United States was increasing its overall level of assistance to fragile and failing states, roughly half of these outlays were destined for three countries: Iraq, Afghanistan, and Pakistan; the remaining 49 fragile states shared a budget request of about $2.6 billion.[322]

The policy of prioritizing aid to institutional performers is an entirely rational one when viewed through the lens of maximizing the effect of donor assistance dollars on growth. However, when viewed through a conflict prevention lens, and taking into account the effectiveness of conflict prevention via development assistance, donor-spending priorities could use some refinement.

The Challenge of Institution Building in Fragile States

The second major challenge in reducing vulnerability to climate conflicts in fragile states is the lack of clear prescriptions for successful institution building in the fragile-state environment. Strengthening institutions is important for several interrelated goals, including economic growth, conflict prevention, and adaptation to climate change. In fragile states, however, international efforts to build such institutional capacity have been vexed by a lack of results. Despite decades of effort, neither academia nor development agencies have yet resolved, in its entirety, the problem of how best to help fragile states build institutions. Acknowledging the lack of full answers, former Inter-American Development Bank Executive Vice President Nancy Birdsall argues that a "weak institutions trap" exists, but that given the major uncertainties over how to overcome it, the first thing for development practitioners to bear in mind is "do no harm."[323]

States trapped by weak institutions are poor and unable to sustain economic growth and development. Among the symptoms of a weak institutions trap that Birdsall enumerates are commodity-export dependency, recent conflict, low non-trade tax revenues, prevalent corruption, and lack of executive accountability.[324]

The lack of qualified personnel in fragile states undermines donor and international community efforts to strengthen their institutions. Tempted to bypass fragile-state institutions to get their programs moving more quickly, donors often use foreign Non-Governmental Organizations (NGOs) or other such intermediaries to implement projects. Using foreign implementing partners, however, does nothing to build governmental capacity, since a significant proportion of the donor funding is spent outside the target country, underwriting the implementer's overhead and salary costs. François and Sud note that, where use of foreign implementing partners is prevalent, local populations can come to view the foreigners, rather than the local government, as service providers.[325] A related strategy, the use of local NGOs or implementing partners, when such exist, also bypasses the local government and additionally causes local partners to hire qualified staff away from the government ministries, actively undermining governmental capacity. Even efforts to build technical capacity in government ministries run into this constraint, as the few persons qualified to train ministry staff are hired away from the upper ranks of the ministries.[326] Birdsall, for example, counsels donors to ensure hiring of implementing partner staff does not come at the expense of limited expertise in local institutions; some donors have experimented with supplementary salary payments to key government personnel to ensure they remain in government employment. Meanwhile, high levels of aid relative to GDP can distort the local labor market and macroeconomy, making it harder for small businesses and exporters to thrive and undermining whatever small middle class may exist in a country.[327]

The development community is still searching for answers for how best to build institutions in fragile states. François and Sud argue that resorting to shortcuts, such as the use of external actors to implement projects, simply undermines local institutions. They argue instead for the use of direct budget support to build capacity incrementally. In their words:

> Ultimately, capacity-building takes place best through gradual 'learning by doing.' Except for the few large and lumpy investments, international assistance should be provided through budget support ... so the state can gradually exercise its most important functions: setting priorities, making hard choices, and managing expenditures. While this may entail the risk of leakage of funds, this risk needs to be viewed against the alternative of the very high administrative costs donors incur in trying to avoid leakages.[328]

Interestingly, this suggestion finds a partial echo in the philosophy adopted by the U.S. Millennium Challenge Account (MCA). While it does not provide direct budget support, the MCA does rely on the grantee government both to propose projects that fit with the country's development priorities, and to administer project implementation.[329] The MCA eligibility criteria, which require meeting certain governance performance thresholds, would make it difficult to give grants to the most fragile states, but the MCA approach nevertheless is one that in principle helps to reinforce institutional capacity. Given the dearth of promising policy alternatives, the international community may well find it makes more sense to engage in such relatively limited, longer-term direct budget support to build fragile state institutional capacity, finance water and agricultural investments, and improve education. Such investments are likely to pay dividends in terms of conflict prevention and increased security.

Structural and Operational Prevention in States with Hybrid Political Orders

A related consideration for the international community acting to build institutional capacity (or state-building) in the fragile state context is the existence of what some researchers have termed "hybrid political orders," where nongovernmental authorities, such as tribal chiefs, coexist with formal governmental structures.[330] In a critique of the state-building paradigm as currently conceived, Debiel and Lambach argue:

Local state-building takes place in hybrid political and societal orders where rival actors of different origin reproduce their power and influence, perform governance functions, or undermine state-building and post-war reconstruction efforts.... In extreme cases of tribal or clan polities, the state is seen as completely distinct and separate space. More common are hybrid situations, in which local actors and powerholders engage with state institutions to advance their own goals.... [E]xternal actors in the pursuit of state-building find themselves negotiating these hybrid political orders. They intervene... without adequately realizing the sociopolitical complexity with which they are faced.[331]

A similar argument is advanced by Boege et al., who advocate taking into account the sorts of hybrid political orders that have emerged in many states the international community defines as fragile. In such places, they note, the state "is only one actor among others, and 'state order' is only one of a number of orders claiming to provide security, frameworks for conflict negotiation and social services."[332]

Such a hybrid political order existed in Darfur, which we explored in Chapter Three. Before 1971, the Sudanese government relied on the system of Tribal Administration to govern Darfur and keep public order. Even after the system's formal removal in 1971, it persisted in weakened form, attempting but ultimately failing to mediate the conflicts that were sparked by climate changes and the 1982–1984 drought and famine. The failure of mediation was a major factor enabling the conflict to escalate. In the parallel case of the Horn of Africa, Meier et al. conclude that resource-related conflicts there have not escalated due to successful mediation and traditional conflict prevention efforts by tribal elders.[333]

The likely existence in many fragile states of such hybrid orders suggests that effective conflict prevention efforts in these states need to flow upward from the local context. In many cases, there will be a clear tension between institution building at the state level and not undermining traditional local conflict mediation institutions. Nevertheless, the two approaches are not necessarily anathema. Boege et al. cite the example of Somaliland. Although officially a part of the failed state of Somalia, Somaliland has built a proto-state and largely maintained peace using the authority of traditional councils of elders, whose role has been formalized in a constitution that also established national authorities along western lines, including a President and Parliament.[334]

The recent research on hybrid political orders does not offer any silver bullet solutions to the question of institution building. Moreover, there will likely always be a tension between the international community's desire to enhance state institutions versus preserving the role of traditional authorities in areas such as conflict mediation. Reconciling those goals will require painstaking work, led by experts on a particular locale, in a bottom-up approach.

Beyond institution building, hybrid political orders will also be challenges for operational conflict prevention efforts. Those seeking to help mitigate tensions and mediate emerging conflicts will need to take into account a much more varied set of actors than exist in many other states. Some of these figures will be potential allies in the cause of conflict prevention, and their roles will need to be thoroughly understood to mobilize their potential contributions.

Will Climate Change Cause Failed States?

Although it seems clear that fragile states are more vulnerable to climate change–related conflicts, the academic literature does not answer whether climate change itself will force fragile states into the more acute condition of state failure, where the state loses the capacity to perform its most basic functions, especially in providing security.

The most comprehensive assessment of state failure conducted to date, that of the State Failure Task Force, found that four simple indicators could predict state failure in 80 percent or more of state failure cases. Out of the Task Force's complicated models with a multiplicity of variables to account for state failure, these four basic indicators were the best predictors of the onset of instability (after a two-year lag). They were the following:

- The presence of internal conflicts in neighboring states.

- A low standard of living, specifically as measured by infant mortality levels.

- Regime type (partial or illiberal democracies are less stable than full democracies or full autocracies).

- The presence of state-led discrimination.[335]

These criteria are not indicators of causality, but rather indicators that the situation in a state is going awry; therefore, they shed limited light on the way in which a force such as climate change relates to the process. It is possible to speculate that climate changes may affect the standard of living of a population, and that this will exacerbate the problem of state failure. Some portions of such a pathway are established in the literature. For example, case studies of drought and its effects on income in Africa suggest that drought has an economic impact and that it is disproportionately felt by the poorest.[336] Separately, this study noted that there was a large but unquantified effect of climate change on the standard of living of the population in Darfur (see Chapter Three). Several reports note that the costs of adapting to climate change will consume scarce resources in states where revenues are limited.[337] State revenues may suffer further due to falling productivity in the agricultural sector, which accounts for a large portion of the economies of many developing countries.[338] Particularly to the extent that such states lack the capacity to make investments toward increasing the adaptive capacity of their agricultural sectors, they may face a vicious cycle of falling revenues further undermining institutional capacity. Although it appears that the variables of climate changes, state failure, and conflicts will all interact, the existing empirical research on state failure ultimately does not settle the question of whether climate change will lead to state failure.

Recommendations

Below are several recommendations for those implementing a strategy for preventing climate change–related conflicts, which flow from the conclusions highlighted in this study.

(1) Focus development spending on building adaptability to climate change in fragile states.

The model developed in the previous chapter and the findings in the conflict prevention literature discussed in this chapter together suggest that development assistance and institution building will have conflict prevention effects. Donor and national government development investments should therefore be focused on projects that increase adaptability to climate change, with highest priority given to those states that vulnerability screens, such as that developed in the previous chapter, suggest are the most vulnerable to such conflicts. Such projects will increase adaptability to climate changes (stage one of the model) through physical infrastructure (water projects, agricultural yields, etc.) and institutional infrastructure (stage two of the model). Such development-oriented interventions have two major advantages: (1) they do not require a great amount of political will to execute and (2) they are much cheaper than dealing with conflicts later.

(2) Rethink spending priorities and fragile state institution building.

Although well motivated and rational, the recent concentration of development program spending on those countries where there is political will and sufficiently strong institutions to meet policy benchmarks has reduced resources available to the most fragile states. Greater development resources need to be devoted to fragile states in order to increase adaptability to climate change and to build institutions. These investments are rational when considered in terms of their cost effectiveness as conflict prevention measures, both operational and structural. Institution building will require extreme patience and a reexamination of ideas such as direct budget support, which had fallen out of favor with many donors but which can be part of an incremental approach to capacity building. Donor patience and long-term approaches are essential.

(3) Adapt conflict prevention strategies to each state.

Each state or country is unique, and the strategies to build institutions will need to reflect that uniqueness. To be effective, institution-building strategies will need to be built on local realities and to recognize the overlapping effects of governance, security, and economic growth on conflict prevention. Institution building will serve those interrelated goals and will pay dividends on several fronts: economic growth, state legitimacy, climate-change adaptation, and conflict prevention and mediation, among others. In principle, institution-building strategies should originate with the country's own leadership, with international community support and direct funding for implementation led by local institutions. This recommendation flows from the discussion of the challenges posed by institution building in fragile states, the need to take account of hybrid political orders, and the finding of the conflict-prevention literature that prevention strategies must be tailored to the particular context.

(4) Avoid undermining traditional conflict prevention.

Where appropriate, institution-building efforts should avoid undermining traditional conflict prevention mechanisms, such as tribal elders. If possible, the traditional mechanisms should be strengthened and connected to broader institution-building efforts at the national and regional level. This recommendation flows from the finding in the Darfur case study that the undermining of traditional conflict mediation in Darfur (and the failure of the Sudanese state effectively to replace them) was a major factor in the escalation of the conflicts created by the 1982–1984 drought and famine.

(5) Implement operational conflict prevention such as mediation and diplomatic interventions early.

Although it is a truism in the conflict prevention world, it bears repeating here that when tensions and simmering conflicts begin to emerge, early intervention is paramount. One intriguing aspect of the Darfur case study was the finding that the conflict was not at first ethnically motivated, but rather was a struggle over water and land necessary to preserve livelihoods. The failure of mediation mechanisms allowed the conflicts to fester, and only then brought to the fore latent ethnic divisions that were, in turn, exploited by conflict entrepreneurs. Effective mediation of the drought-related conflicts also likely would have stopped the subsequent escalation into ethnically motivated mass killings. It bears reiteration that, when executed in the initial stages of a conflict, interventions can be very limited in scope and executed by institutions already on the ground, such as representatives of multilateral or regional organizations or even bilateral diplomatic missions. Such limited-scale preventive interventions require substantially less political will from the international community.

(6) Respond to climatic disasters quickly.

In case of extreme weather events, early humanitarian response, including by the military or peacekeeping units, may help keep the migration cycle in check and head off resulting political instability. A large statistical study by Nel and Righarts, covering the period 1950–2000, showed that rapid-onset natural disasters, a category that includes typhoons, earthquakes, floods, and mudslides, were associated with a significant risk of subsequent violent internal conflict.[339] As Schwartz notes: "[T]he only difference between the collapse of civil order and a failed state is whether order is eventually restored."[340] This recommendation also flows from the observation in the Darfur case study that failure of the government to provide relief to those affected by the 1982–1984 drought played a role in the escalation of that conflict.

(7) Confront conflict entrepreneurs.

Aggressively confronting the conflict discourse of xenophobic politicians and other conflict entrepreneurs can help short-circuit the fear, blame, and violence that the conflict entrepreneurs seek to institute. This is best done by local leaders and elites, but the international community should not stand by if local leaders fail to do so. This recommendation flows from the findings on the role of conflict entrepreneurs in conflict escalation explored in Chapter Four.

(8) Compile better information.

There is a need for better information and intelligence on conflicts and potential conflicts, particularly when these are in their incipient stages. Only limited information made its way to the international community on the conflicts in Darfur in the 1980s and 1990s, such as the 1987–1989 Arab-Fur war and the 1996–1999 Arab-Masalit war. These conflicts produced thousands of fatalities and widespread atrocities, with relatively little reporting or awareness outside Sudan. Many early warning networks that monitor for such conflicts have since been built, but this remains an area upon which the international community could improve.

(9) Lack of political will: do not write off difficult cases such as Darfur.

Darfur stands as a stark reminder of how unmet human needs and festering conflicts can escalate, with disastrous consequences. The tragedy in Darfur was worsened by the complicity of the Sudanese government in atrocities and a lack of political will in the international community to intervene militarily. When there is a lack of political will to intervene with force, then there is an even greater imperative for the international community to continue operational conflict-prevention interventions, as well as ensuring that humanitarian assistance and efforts to restore livelihoods continue. Doing so has and will have conflict-mitigation effects, even though these may be overwhelmed by the scale of the conflict in question. In addition, the humanitarian networks put in place in such cases will help the international community play a mediation role as well. But it must be recognized that, at this stage, the sort of interventions discussed in this study will be ineffectual without serious political will from both the international community and local authorities.

Conclusion

Building adaptability to climate change through development projects and institution building has the great advantage of simultaneously serving both development and conflict-prevention goals. Such efforts serve these goals by disrupting the pathways through which intermediate level climate changes create the potential for conflict. Combined with the tools of operational conflict prevention, such as preventive diplomacy and mediation, the international community has a range of options to deploy to reduce the risk of climate change–related conflicts. Such preventive adaptation to climate change should become a mantra for the international community in fragile states.

These sorts of limited, preventive interventions have the great advantage of only demanding relatively limited political will and expenditures, particularly as compared with peacekeeping or other forceful international intervention. Even where situations deteriorate into conflict, such as Darfur, addressing the underlying needs for secure livelihoods is always a necessary part of a lasting solution to the types of conflict that climate change may spark.

As part of current global climate negotiations, there has been agreement for significant resource transfer to developing nations to begin addressing problems of adaptation. Those resources represent an invaluable opportunity to integrate cost-effective conflict prevention planning into the adaptation agenda. It is an opportunity we miss at our peril.

Figure 18: Stages of Policy Response

Stage	Indicators	Time-line	Types of Actions	Implementers
Structural prevention through adaptation	Vulnerability assessments, World Bank assistance strategies	Years to months before a potential conflict	Investments in wells, water catchment, and irrigation; agricultural productivity improvements	National and local governments, supported by development agencies, bilateral donors, NGOs
Structural prevention through institutional strength-ening	Assessments of institutional strength	Years to months before conflict	Institution building, role of local conflict-resolution mechanisms, tolerance education	National and local governments, development agencies, bilateral donors, NGOs
Operational prevention	Heightened political rhetoric emphasizing group divisions, isolated violence, crop failures, extreme weather events, refugee flows	Months to days before conflict	Mediation, confidence-building measures, outreach to problematic political leaders, public diplomacy, relief operations	UN, regional organizations such as OSCE or AU, bilateral embassies, working with local authorities where possible
Crisis management	Outbreak of generalized violence	During violence	Negotiations, relief operations, peace-keepers	UN, regional organizations, bilateral embassies, peace-keepers, military

About the Author

J. Andrew Plowman is a career U.S. Foreign Service Officer. His service with the State Department has included assignments to Peru, Panama, Kazakhstan, and Brazil, as well as Washington assignments with the Bureau of European and Eurasian Affairs and the Economics, Energy, and Business Affairs Bureau.

Mr. Plowman is a 1990 graduate of Cornell College in Iowa, where he earned a Bachelor's Degree in History and International Relations. He obtained a Master of Arts from the International Policy program at Stanford University in 2003.

Notes

Chapter One

1. CNA Corporation, *National Security and the Threat of Climate Change* (Alexandria, VA: The CNA Corporation, 2007); German Advisory Council on Global Change, *Climate Change as a Security Risk* (London and Sterling, VA: Earthscan, 2008).

2. Kurt Campbell, ed., *Climatic Cataclysm: The Foreign Policy and National Security Implications of Climate Change* (Washington DC: Brookings Institution Press, 2008).

3. Geoffrey D. Dabelko, "Avoid Hyperbole, Oversimplification when Climate and Security Meet," in *Bulletin of the Atomic Scientists* 15, no. 7 (August 24, 2009), http://thebulletin.org/avoid-hyperbole-oversimplification-when-climate-and-security-meet; Oli Brown, Anne Hammill, and Robert McLeman, "Climate Change as the 'New' Security Threat: Implications for Africa," *International Affairs* 83, no. 6 (2007): 1141–1154.

4. Susan Solomon et al., "IPCC 2007: The Physical Science Basis," in *Contribution of Working Group I to the Fourth Assessment Report of the Intergovernmental Panel on Climate Change*, ed. Susan Solomon et al. (Cambridge, UK, and New York, NY: Cambridge University Press, 2007); Richard B. Alley et al., "IPCC 2007: Summary for Policymakers," in *Contribution of Working Group I to the Fourth Assessment Report of the Intergovernmental Panel on Climate Change*, ed. Susan Solomon et al. (Cambridge, UK, and New York, NY: Cambridge University Press, 2007).

5. Malcolm Chalmers, "Spending to Save? An Analysis of the Cost Effectiveness of Conflict Prevention versus Intervention After the Onset of Violent Conflict: Phase 2 Synthesis Report," Working Papers (Bradford, UK: Bradford University, 2005).

6. National Security Council, *National Security Strategy* (Washington, DC: U.S. Government Printing Office, 2010); National Security Council, *The National Security Strategy of the United States of America* (Washington, DC: U.S. Government Printing Office, 2006); National Security Council, *The National Security Strategy of the United States of America* (Washington, DC: U.S. Government Printing Office, 2002).

7. CNA Corporation, *National Security*; German Advisory Council on Global Change, *Security Risk*; Dan Smith and Janani Vivekananda, "A Climate of Conflict: The Links between Climate Change, Peace and War," *International Alert* (London, 2007).

8. Thomas F. Homer-Dixon, "Environmental Scarcities and Violent Conflict: Evidence from Cases," *International Security* 19, no. 1 (1994): 5–40.

9. Wenche Hauge and Tanja Ellingsen, "Beyond Environmental Scarcity: Causal Pathways to Conflict," *Journal of Peace Research* 35, no. 3 (1998): 299.

10. Thomas Homer-Dixon, "Positive Feedbacks, Dynamic Ice Sheets, and the Recarbonization of the Global Fuel Supply: The New Sense of Urgency about Global Warming," in *A Globally Integrated Climate Policy for Canada*, ed. Steven Bernstein et al. (Toronto: University of Toronto Press, 2007), 37–54; Thomas Homer-Dixon, "Straw Man in the Wind," *The National Interest* Jan/Feb 2008, no. 93 (2008): 26.

11. Homer-Dixon, "Environmental Scarcities," 5–40.

12. Nils Petter Gleditsch et al., "Conflicts Over Shared Rivers: Resource Scarcity Or Fuzzy Boundaries?," *Political Geography* 25 (2006): 361–382; Helga Malmin Binningsbø, Indra de Soysa, and Nils Petter Gleditsch, "Green Giant Or Straw Man? Environmental Pressure and Civil Conflict, 1961–99," *Population and Environment* 28, no. 6 (2007): 337–353; Ole Magnus Theisen, "Other Pathways to Conflict? Environmental Scarcities and Domestic Conflict" (paper presented at the 47th Annual Convention of the International Studies Association, San Diego, CA, March 22–25, 2006); Clionadh Raleigh and Henrik Urdal, "Climate Change, Environmental Degradation and Armed Conflict," *Political Geography* 26 (2007): 674–694; Nils Petter Gleditsch et al., "Armed Conflict 1946–2001: A New Dataset," *Journal of Peace Research* 39, no. 5 (2002): 615–637.

13. Halvard Buhaug, Nils Petter Gleditsch, and Ole Magnus Theisen, "Implications of Climate Change for Armed Conflict" (The World Bank, "Social Dimensions of Climate Change" workshop, Washington, DC, March 5–6, 2008).

14. Ole Magnus Theisen, "Blood and Soil? Resource Scarcity and Internal Armed Conflict Revisited," *Journal of Peace Research* 45, no. 6 (2008): 801.

15. Raleigh and Urdal, "Environmental Degradation," 674–694.

16. Edward Miguel, Shanker Satyanath, and Ernest Sergenti, "Economic Shocks and Civil Conflict: An Instrumental Variables Approach," *Journal of Political Economy* 112, no. 4 (2004): 725.

17. Cullen S. Hendrix and Sarah M. Glaser, "Trends and Triggers: Climate, Climate Change and Civil Conflict in Sub-Saharan Africa," *Political Geography* 26 (2007): 695–715.

18. Marc A. Levy et al., "Freshwater Availability Anomalies and Outbreak of Internal War: Results from a Global Spatial Time Series Analysis" (paper presented at the Human Security and Climate Change International Workshop, Holmen Fjord Hotel, Asker, near Oslo, June 21–23, 2005).

19. David D. Zhang et al., "Climatic Change, Wars and Dynastic Cycles in China Over the Last Millennium," *Climatic Change* 76 (2006): 459–477.

20. Richard S. J. Tol and Sebastian Wagner, "Climate Change and Violent Conflict in Europe Over the Last Millennium," *Climatic Change* 99, no. 1–2 (2010), http://dx.doi.org/10.1007/s10584-009-9659-2.

21. Patrick D. Nunn, "The A.D. 1300 Event in the Pacific Basin," *The Geographical Review* 97, no. 1 (2007): 1–23.

22. Jared Diamond, *Collapse: How Societies Choose to Fail Or Succeed* (New York: Penguin Books, 2006).

23. Idean Salehyan, "From Climate Change to Conflict? No Consensus Yet," *Journal of Peace Research* 45, no. 3 (2008): 315.

24. Halvard Buhaug and Päivi Lujala, "Accounting for Scale: Measuring Geography in Quantitative Studies of Civil War," *Political Geography* 24, no. 4 (2005): 399–418.

25. Hauge and Ellingsen, "Beyond Environmental Scarcity," 299.

26. Jon Barnett and W. Neil Adger, "Climate Change, Human Security and Violent Conflict," *Political Geography* 26 (2007): 639–655.

27. Organization for Security and Cooperation in Europe, Factsheet, "What is the OSCE?," April 29, 2013, http://www.osce.org/secretariat/35775.

28. Neil Leary and Jyoti Kulkarni, "Climate Change Vulnerability and Adaptation in Developing Country Regions" (Washington, DC: The International START Secretariat, and Trieste, Italy: The Academy of Sciences for the Developing World, 2007).

29. Joyce R. Starr, "Water Wars," *Foreign Policy* 82 (Spring 1991): 17–36.

30. Peter H. Gleick, "Water and Conflict: Fresh Water Resources and International Security," *International Security* 18, no. 1 (Summer 1993): 79–112; Peter H. Gleick, Ashbindu Singh, and Hua Shi, *Emerging Threats to the World's*

Freshwater Resources (Oakland, CA: Pacific Institute for Studies in Development, Environment, and Security, 2002); German Advisory Council on Global Change, *Security Risk.*

31. Shira Yoffe, Aaron T. Wolf, and Mark Giordano, "Conflict and Cooperation Over International Freshwater Resources: Indicators of Basins at Risk," *Journal of the American Water Resources Association* 39, no. 5 (2003): 1109–1126.

32. Aaron T. Wolf et al., "Water Can be a Pathway to Peace, Not War," *Navigating Peace 1* (Woodrow Wilson International Center for Scholars, 2006).

33. Gleditsch et al., "Conflicts Over Shared Rivers," 361–382.

34. Andrea K. Gerlak and Keith A. Grant, "The Correlates of Cooperative Institutions for International Rivers," in *Mapping the New World Order*, ed. Thomas J. Volgy et al. (Malden, MA: Wiley-Blackwell, 2009), 114–147.

35. Yoffe, Wolf, and Giordano, "Conflict and Cooperation"; Mark Zeitoun and Naho Mirumachi, "Transboundary Water Interaction I: Reconsidering Conflict and Cooperation," *International Environmental Agreements: Politics, Law & Economics* 8, no. 4 (2008): 297–316.

36. Tom M. L. Wigley et al., "Implications of Proposed CO_2 Emissions Limitations," Technical Paper 4, Intergovernmental Panel on Climate Change (1997); David A. Randall et al., "Climate Models and their Evaluation," in *Climate Change 2007: The Physical Science Basis; Contribution of Working Group I to the Fourth Assessment Report of the Intergovernmental Panel on Climate Change*, ed. Susan Solomon et al. (Cambridge, UK, and New York, NY: Cambridge University Press, 2007); Gerald A. Meehl et al., "Global Climate Projections," in *Climate Change 2007: The Physical Science Basis; Contribution of Working Group I to the Fourth Assessment Report of the Intergovernmental Panel on Climate Change*, ed. Susan Solomon et al. (Cambridge, UK, and New York, NY: Cambridge University Press, 2007); Michel Boko et al., "Africa: Impacts, Adaptation and Vulnerability," in *Climate Change 2007: Impacts, Adaptation and Vulnerability; Contribution of Working Group II to the Fourth Assessment Report of the Intergovernmental Panel on Climate Change* (Cambridge, UK: Cambridge University Press, 2007), 433–467.

Chapter Two

37. Naomi Oreskes, "Beyond the Ivory Tower: The Scientific Consensus on Climate Change," *Science* 306, no. 5702 (December 2004): 1686.

38. American Association for the Advancement of Science et al., "Statement on Climate Change from 18 Scientific Associations," Letter to Congress, October 21, 2009, http://www.ucsusa.org/ssi/climate-change/scientific-consensus-on.html.

39. The National Academies, "Joint Science Academies' Statement: Global Response to Climate Change," http://www.nationalacademies.org/onpi/06072005.pdf, 2005.

40. Alley et al., "Summary for Policymakers."

41. Meehl et al., "Global Climate Projections"; Alley et al., "Summary for Policymakers."

42. Randall et al., "Climate Models and their Evaluation"; Wigley et al., "Implications of Proposed CO_2 Emissions Limitations."

43. Solomon et al., "The Physical Science Basis."

44. Joseph F. C. DiMento and Pamela Doughman, eds., *Climate Change: What It Means for Us, Our Children, and Our Grandchildren* (Cambridge, MA: MIT Press, 2007).

45. United Nations Intergovernmental Panel on Climate Change, *Climate Change 2001: IPCC Third Assessment Report,* http://www.grida.no/publications/other/ipcc_tar/.

46. Alley et al., "Summary for Policymakers."

47. Bryson Bates et al., eds., *Climate Change and Water* (Geneva: IPCC Secretariat, 2008); Timothy R. Carter et al., "New Assessment Methods and the Characterisation of Future Conditions," in *Climate Change 2007: Impacts, Adaptation and Vulnerability; Contribution of Working Group II to the Fourth Assessment Report of the Intergovernmental Panel on Climate Change,* ed. Martin Parry et al. (Cambridge, UK: Cambridge University Press, 2007), 133–171.

48. Bates et al., *Climate Change and Water.*

49. Ibid.

50. Jens Hesselbjerg Christensen et al., "IPCC 2007: Regional Climate Projections," in *Contribution of Working Group I to the Fourth Assessment Report of the Intergovernmental Panel on Climate Change,* ed. Susan Solomon et al. (Cambridge, UK, and New York, NY: Cambridge University Press, 2007).

51. The World Bank, *World Development Report 2010: Development and Climate Change* (Washington, DC: The World Bank, 2010).

52. International Food Policy Research Institute (IFPRI), *Climate Change: Impact on Agriculture and Costs of Adaptation*, ed. Gerald C. Nelson et al. (Washington, DC: International Food Policy Research Institute, 2009).

53. Ibid.

54. Ibid.; Karen O'Brien et al., "Mapping Vulnerability to Multiple Stressors: Climate Change and Globalization in India," *Global Environmental Change* 14, no. 4 (2004): 303–313.

55. "Hunger is the Lack of Rain," Newsroom, United Nations Development Programme, accessed December 1, 2009, http://content.undp.org/go/newsroom/2009/november/hunger-is-the-lack-of-rain.en.

56. IFPRI, *Climate Change: Impact on Agriculture*; United Nations, Department of Economic and Social Affairs, Population Division, *World Population Prospects: The 2008 Revision* (New York, NY: United Nations, 2009).

57. IFPRI, *Climate Change: Impact on Agriculture.*

58. The World Bank, *World Development Report 2008: Agriculture for Development* (Washington, DC: The World Bank, 2007).

59. Anthony Okon Nyong, "Climate Change, Agriculture and Trade: Implications for Sustainable Development" (paper prepared for the International Centre for Trade and Sustainable Development [ICTSD] and the session titled "Agriculture, Climate Change and Sustainable Development" at The Future of Agriculture: A Global Dialogue amongst Stakeholders, Barcelona, May 30–31, 2008).

60. Mike Davis, *Late Victorian Holocausts: El Niño Famines and the Making of the Third World* (London: Verso Books, 2001).

61. Ibid.

62. Robert W. Sutherst, "Global Change and Human Vulnerability to Vector-Borne Diseases," *Clinical Microbiology Reviews* 17, no. 1 (January 2004): 136–173.

63. Ulisses Confalonieri et al., "Human Health," in *Climate Change 2007: Impacts, Adaptation and Vulnerability; Contribution of Working Group II to the Fourth*

Assessment Report of the Intergovernmental Panel on Climate Change, ed. Martin Parry et al. (Cambridge, UK: Cambridge University Press, 2007), 391–431.

64. Sutherst, "Global Change and Human Vulnerability."

65. Matthew H. Bonds et al., "Poverty Trap Formed by the Ecology of Infectious Diseases," *Proceedings of the Royal Society B* (December 9, 2009), http://dx.doi.org/10.1098/rspb.2009.1778.

66. Commission on Macroeconomics and Health, *Macroeconomics and Health: Investing in Health for Economic Development* (Geneva, Switzerland: World Health Organization, 2001); World Health Organization, *The World Health Report 2004: Changing History* (Geneva, Switzerland: World Health Organization, 2004).

67. Meehl et al., "Global Climate Projections"; Robert J. Nicholls et al., "Coastal Systems and Low-Lying Areas," in *Climate Change 2007: Impacts, Adaptation and Vulnerability; Contribution of Working Group II to the Fourth Assessment Report of the Intergovernmental Panel on Climate Change*, ed. Martin Parry et al. (Cambridge, UK: Cambridge University Press, 2007), 315–356; Radley Horton et al., "Sea Level Rise Projections for Current Generation CGCMs Based on the Semi-Empirical Method," *Geophysical Research Letters* 35, no. L02715 (2008).

68. Susmita Dasgupta et al., "The Impact of Sea Level Rise on Developing Countries: A Comparative Analysis" (Washington, DC: The World Bank, 2007).

69. Ibid.

70. CNA Corporation, *National Security*; German Advisory Council on Global Change, Security Risk.

Chapter Three

71. U.S. Department of State, "Background Note: Sudan," accessed March 17, 2010, originally published at http://www.state.gov/r/pa/ei/bgn/5424.htm; Olivier Degomme and Debarati Guha-Sapir, "Patterns of Mortality Rates in Darfur Conflict," *The Lancet* 375, no. 9711 (2010): 294–300.

72. The International Criminal Court, "Fourth Report of the Prosecutor of the International Criminal Court, Mr. Luis Moreno Ocampo, to the UN Security Council Pursuant to UNSCR 1593 (2005)," December 14, 2006, http://www.icc-cpi.int/NR/rdonlyres/19B2F772-E5E3-4DBB-8B0F-5A220DB958F3/277803/OTP_ReportUNSC4Darfur_English.pdf.

73. Alex de Waal, "Famine Mortality: A Case Study of Darfur, Sudan 1984–5," *Population Studies* 43, no. 1 (1989): 5–24.

74. Abdalla Ahmed Abdalla, "Environmental Degradation and Conflict in Darfur: Experiences and Development Options," in Conference Proceedings, *Environmental Degradation as a Cause of Conflict in Darfur* (Addis Ababa, Ethiopia: University for Peace, Africa Programme, 2006).

75. De Waal, "Famine Mortality," 5–24.

76. Noah R. Bassil, "The Rise and Demise of the Keira Sultanate of Dar Fur," *Journal of North African Studies* 11, no. 4 (2006): 347–364; Julie Flint and Alex de Waal, *Darfur: A New History of a Long War* (London and New York, NY: Zed Books Ltd, 2008).

77. Rex Sean O'Fahey, "Conflict in Darfur: Historical and Contemporary Perspectives," in Conference Proceedings, *Environmental Degradation as a Cause of Conflict in Darfur* (Addis Ababa, Ethiopia: University for Peace, Africa Programme, 2006).

78. Alex de Waal, "Who are the Darfurians? Arab and African Identities, Violence and External Engagement," *African Affairs* 104, no. 415 (2005): 181.

79. Rex Sean O'Fahey, *The Darfur Sultanate: A History* (New York, NY: Columbia University Press, 2008).

80. Flint and de Waal, *Darfur: A New History of a Long War.*

81. Bassil, "The Rise and Demise of the Keira Sultanate of Dar Fur," 347–364.

82. Ibid.

83. Ibid.

84. Ibid.

85. Martin W. Daly, *Darfur's Sorrow: The Forgotten History of a Humanitarian Disaster* (Cambridge, UK, and New York, NY: Cambridge University Press, 2010).

86. Robert O. Collins, *A History of Modern Sudan* (Cambridge, UK, and New York, NY: Cambridge University Press, 2008).

87. Arthur E. Robinson, "The Arab Dynasty of Dar for (Darfur) A. D. 1448–1874 Or A. H. 852–1201: Part I," *Journal of the Royal African Society* 27, no. 108 (July 1928): 353–363.

88. Collins, *A History of Modern Sudan*; Flint and de Waal, *Darfur: A New History of a Long War*.

89. Flint and de Waal, *Darfur: A New History of a Long War*.

90. Erik Solevad Nielsen, "Ethnic Boundaries and Conflict in Darfur: An Event Structure Hypothesis," *Ethnicities* 8, no. 4 (December 2008): 427–462; Flint and de Waal, *Darfur: A New History of a Long War*.

91. De Waal, "Who are the Darfurians?," 181.

92. Nielsen, "Ethnic Boundaries," 427–462; Abdalla, "Environmental Degradation"; Flint and de Waal, *Darfur: A New History of a Long War*.

93. Ibid.

94. O'Fahey, "Conflict in Darfur"; Nielsen, "Ethnic Boundaries," 427–462.

95. Flint and de Waal, *Darfur: A New History of a Long War*; O'Fahey, "Conflict in Darfur."

96. Flint and de Waal, *Darfur: A New History of a Long War*.

97. Nielsen, "Ethnic Boundaries," 427–462; de Waal, "Who are the Darfurians?," 181.

98. Flint and de Waal, *Darfur: A New History of a Long War*.

99. Fredrik Barth, *Human Resources: Social and Cultural Features of the Jebel Marra Project Area; Bergen Studies in Social Anthropology* (Bergen, Norway: Department of Social Anthropology, University of Bergen, 1988).

100. Nielsen, "Ethnic Boundaries," 427–462; de Waal, "Who are the Darfurians?," 181.

101. Flint and de Waal, *Darfur: A New History of a Long War*.

102. Ibid.

103. Nielsen, "Ethnic Boundaries," 427–462.

104. Bassil, "The Rise and Demise of the Keira Sultanate of Dar Fur," 347–364.

105. De Waal, "Who are the Darfurians?," 181.

106. Flint and de Waal, *Darfur: A New History of a Long War.*

107. Paul Doornbos, "On Becoming Sudanese: Aspects of Ideological Transformation in Rural Sudan," paper presented at the Workshop on Capital, State, and Transformation in Sudan, ed. Tony Barnett and Abbas Abdelkarim (London: Croom Helm, 1988): 99–121.

108. Sharif Harir, "'Arab Belt' Versus 'African Belt': Ethno-Political Conflict in Dar Fur and the Regional Cultural Factors," in *Shortcut to Decay: The Case of Sudan*, eds. Sharif Harir and Terje Tvedt (Motala, Sweden: Nordiska Afrikainstitutet, 1994), 144–185.

109. Flint and de Waal, *Darfur: A New History of a Long War.*

110. Julie Flint and Alex de Waal, "Case Closed: A Prosecutor without Borders," *World Affairs* 171, no. 4 (Spring 2009): 23–38.

111. De Waal, "Who are the Darfurians?," 181.

112. Flint and de Waal, *Darfur: A New History of a Long War*; O'Fahey, "Conflict in Darfur."

113. Nielsen, "Ethnic Boundaries," 427–462.

114. Flint and de Waal, *Darfur: A New History of a Long War.*

115. Collins, *A History of Modern Sudan.*

116. Ibid.; de Waal, "Who are the Darfurians?," 181.

117. Flint and de Waal, *Darfur: A New History of a Long War.*

118. Ibid.

119. Adam Azzain Mohamed, "Indigenous Institutions and Practices Promoting Peace and/or Mitigating Conflicts: The Case of Southern Darfur of Western Sudan," in Conference Proceedings, *Environmental Degradation as a Cause of Conflict in Darfur* (Addis Ababa, Ethiopia: University for Peace, Africa Programme, 2006).

120. Nielsen, "Ethnic Boundaries," 427–462.

121. De Waal, "Who are the Darfurians?," 181.

122. Nielsen, "Ethnic Boundaries," 427–462.

123. O'Fahey, "Conflict in Darfur."

124. Ibid.; Flint and de Waal, *Darfur: A New History of a Long War.*

125. Z. M. Bashar, "Mechanisms for Peaceful Co-Existence among Tribal Groups in Darfur" (master's thesis, University of Khartoum, 2003); United Nations Environment Programme, *Sudan: Post-Conflict Environmental Assessment* (Nairobi, Kenya: United Nations Environment Programme, 2007).

126. Harir, "'Arab Belt' Versus 'African Belt,'" 144–185.

127. Ibid.

128. De Waal, "Who are the Darfurians?," 181.

129. Scott Edwards, "Social Breakdown in Darfur," *Forced Migration Review* 31 (October 2008): 23.

130. Serigne Tacko Kandji, Louis Verchot, and Jens Mackensen, *Climatic Change and Variability in the Sahel Region: Impacts and Adaptation Strategies in the Agricultural Sector* (Nairobi, Kenya: United Nations Environment Programme and the World Agroforestry Centre, 2006).

131. Michael Kevane and Leslie Gray, "Darfur: Rainfall and Conflict," *Environmental Research Letters* 3 (2008): 034006.

132. Ibid.

133. Marcel Leroy, ed., *Environment and Conflict in Africa: Reflections on Darfur* (Addis Ababa, Ethiopia: University for Peace, Africa Programme, 2009).

134. Mary King and Mohamed Awad Osman, "Executive Summary," in Conference Proceedings, *Environmental Degradation as a Cause of Conflict in Darfur* (Addis Ababa, Ethiopia: University for Peace, Africa Programme, 2006); United Nations Environment Programme, *Sudan: Post-Conflict Environmental Assessment.*

135. Ibid.

136. O'Fahey, "Conflict in Darfur."

137. United Nations Environment Programme, *Sudan: Post-Conflict Environmental Assessment*; Nielsen, "Ethnic Boundaries," 427–462.

138. Lennart Olsson and Mryka Hall-Beyer, "Greening of the Sahel," in *Encyclopedia of Earth*, ed. Cutler J. Cleveland (Washington, DC: Environmental Information Coalition, National Council for Science and the Environment, 2008); Fana Gebresenbet, "Climate and Vegetation Changes in the Sahel: The Case of Darfur," in *Environment and Conflict in Africa: Reflections on Darfur*, ed. Marcel Leroy (Addis Ababa, Ethiopia: University for Peace, Africa Programme, 2009), 14–26.

139. Martin L. Parry et al., eds., *Climate Change 2007: Impacts, Adaptation and Vulnerability; Contribution of Working Group II to the Fourth Assessment Report of the Intergovernmental Panel on Climate Change* (Cambridge, UK: Cambridge University Press, 2007).

140. United Nations Environment Programme, *Sudan: Post-Conflict Environmental Assessment*.

141. Kevane and Gray, "Darfur: Rainfall and Conflict," 034006.

142. United Nations Environment Programme, *Sudan: Post-Conflict Environmental Assessment*; de Waal, "Who are the Darfurians?," 181; Nielsen, "Ethnic Boundaries," 427–462.

143. Flint and de Waal, *Darfur: A New History of a Long War*.

144. Nielsen, "Ethnic Boundaries," 427–462.

145. O'Fahey, "Conflict in Darfur."

146. Abdalla, "Environmental Degradation"; Flint and de Waal, *Darfur: A New History of a Long War*; O'Fahey, "Conflict in Darfur."

147. Abdelkrim Ben Mohamed, Niek van Duivenbooden, and Saidou Abdoussallam, "Impact of Climate Change on Agricultural Production in the Sahel—Part 1; Methodological Approach and Case Study for Millet in Niger," *Climatic Change* 54, no. 3 (August 1, 2002): 327–348.

148. Nielsen, "Ethnic Boundaries," 427–462.

149. De Waal, "Famine Mortality," 5–24.

150. Tesfaye Teklu, Joachim Von Braun, and Elsayed Ali Ahmed Zaki, *Drought and Famine Relationships in Sudan: Policy Implications* (Washington, DC: International Food Policy Research Institute, 1991).

151. De Waal, "Famine Mortality," 5–24.

152. Flint and de Waal, *Darfur: A New History of a Long War.*

153. Harir, "'Arab Belt' Versus 'African Belt,'" 144–185.

154. Nielsen, "Ethnic Boundaries," 427–462.

155. Alex de Waal, "Is Climate Change the Culprit for Darfur?," *African Arguments* (blog), June 25, 2007, accessed February 2010, http://africanarguments.org/2007/06/25/is-climate-change-the-culprit-for-darfur/.

156. Collins, *A History of Modern Sudan.*

157. Ibid.; Abdalla, "Environmental Degradation"; O'Fahey, "Conflict in Darfur."

158. Flint and de Waal, *Darfur: A New History of a Long War.*

159. Ibid.

160. Ibid.

161. Ibid.

162. Collins, *A History of Modern Sudan.*

163. Ibid.; Flint and de Waal, *Darfur: A New History of a Long War.*

164. Ibid.; Collins, *A History of Modern Sudan.*

165. Flint and de Waal, *Darfur: A New History of a Long War.*

166. O'Fahey, "Conflict in Darfur"; Flint and de Waal, *Darfur: A New History of a Long War.*

167. Flint and de Waal, Darfur: *A New History of a Long War.*

168. O'Fahey, "Conflict in Darfur."

169. J. Millard Burr and Robert O. Collins, *Africa's Thirty Years' War: Libya, Chad and the Sudan, 1963–1993* (Boulder, CO: Westview Press, 1999).

170. Collins, *A History of Modern Sudan;* Flint and de Waal, *Darfur: A New History of a Long War.*

171. Ibid.

172. Collins, *A History of Modern Sudan.*

173. Harir, "'Arab Belt' Versus 'African Belt,'" 144–185.

174. Nielsen, "Ethnic Boundaries," 427–462; Collins, *A History of Modern Sudan*; Flint and de Waal, *Darfur: A New History of a Long War.*

175. Harir, "'Arab Belt' Versus 'African Belt,'" 144–185; Flint and de Waal, *Darfur: A New History of a Long War.*

176. Harir, "'Arab Belt' Versus 'African Belt,'" 144–185.

177. Ibid.

178. Ibid.

179. Ibid.

180. Ibid.

181. Ibid.

182. Flint and de Waal, *Darfur: A New History of a Long War.*

183. Harir, "'Arab Belt' Versus 'African Belt,'" 144–185.

184. Flint and de Waal, *Darfur: A New History of a Long War.*

185. Harir, "'Arab Belt' Versus 'African Belt,'" 144–185.

186. O'Fahey, "Conflict in Darfur."

187. Mahmood Mamdani, "'There May have been No Water, but the Province was Awash with Guns,'" *New Statesman* 138, no. 4952 (2009): 34–37.

188. John Hagan and Wenona Rymond-Richmond, *Darfur and the Crime of Genocide* (Cambridge, UK: Cambridge University Press, 2008).

189. De Waal, "Who are the Darfurians?," 181.

190. Flint and de Waal, *Darfur: A New History of a Long War.*

191. Ibid.

CLIMATE CHANGE AND CONFLICT PREVENTION

192. Harir, "'Arab Belt' Versus 'African Belt,'" 144–185.

193. Flint and de Waal, *Darfur: A New History of a Long War.*

194. Ibid.

195. Ibid.

196. United Nations Environment Programme, *Sudan: Post-Conflict Environmental Assessment.*

197. Flint and de Waal, *Darfur: A New History of a Long War;* Collins, *A History of Modern Sudan.*

198. Flint and de Waal, *Darfur: A New History of a Long War.*

199. Ibid.

200. Ibid.; Collins, *A History of Modern Sudan;* O'Fahey, "Conflict in Darfur."

201. Collins, *A History of Modern Sudan;* Flint and de Waal, *Darfur: A New History of a Long War.*

202. U.S. Department of State, "Background Note: Sudan."

203. Degomme and Guha-Sapir, "Patterns of Mortality Rates in Darfur Conflict," 294–300; U.S. Department of State, "Background Note: Sudan."

204. Mamdani, "'There May have been No Water, but the Province was Awash with Guns,'" 34–37.

205. Flint and de Waal, *Darfur: A New History of a Long War.*

206. Dennis J. D. Sandole, "Virulent Ethnocentrism: A Major Challenge for Transformational Conflict Resolution and Peacebuilding in the Post–Cold War Era," *Ethnopolitics* 1, no. 4 (2002): 4–27.

207. Bassil, "The Rise and Demise of the Keira Sultanate of Dar Fur," 347–364.

208. Harir, "'Arab Belt' Versus 'African Belt,'" 144–185.

209. Syed Mansoob Murshed, "The Conflict-Growth Nexus and the Poverty of Nations," United Nations Department of Economics and Social Affairs Working Paper No. 43 (June 2007).

133

210. Flint and de Waal, *Darfur: A New History of a Long War.*

211. Eltigani E. Eltigani, ed., *War and Drought in Sudan: Essays on Population Displacement* (Gainesville, FL: University Press of Florida, 1995).

212. Flint and de Waal, *Darfur: A New History of a Long War.*

213. Nielsen, "Ethnic Boundaries," 427–462.

214. Barth, *Human Resources.*

215. Nielsen, "Ethnic Boundaries," 427–462.

216. Flint and de Waal, *Darfur: A New History of a Long War.*

217. Kevane and Gray, "Darfur: Rainfall and Conflict," 034006.

218. United Nations Environment Programme, *Sudan: Post-Conflict Environmental Assessment.*

219. Kevane and Gray, "Darfur: Rainfall and Conflict," 034006; Miguel, Satyanath, and Sergenti, "Economic Shocks and Civil Conflict," 725.

220. Kevane and Gray, "Darfur: Rainfall and Conflict," 034006.

221. Teklu, Von Braun, and Zaki, *Drought and Famine.*

222. Alex de Waal, "Darfur: The Inside Story," *New African* 461 (April 2007): 28–33.

223. Hendrix and Glaser, "Trends and Triggers," 695–715.

224. Ban Ki Moon, "A Climate Culprit in Darfur," Opinion, *Washington Post*, June 16, 2007.

225. Stephan Faris, "The Real Roots of Darfur," *Atlantic*, April 2007.

226. Alessandra Giannini, Michela Biasutti, and Michel M. Verstraete, "A Climate Model-Based Review of Drought in the Sahel: Desertification, the Re-Greening and Climate Change," *Global and Planetary Change* 64, no. 3–4 (December 2008): 119–128.

227. Ibid.

228. Ban, "A Climate Culprit in Darfur."

Chapter Four

229. Flint and de Waal, *Darfur: A New History of a Long War*; Nielsen, "Ethnic Boundaries," 427–462; Barnett and Adger, "Climate Change, Human Security and Violent Conflict," 639–655; Kalevi J. Holsti, *The State, War, and the State of War* (Cambridge, UK: Cambridge University Press, 1996); Homer-Dixon, "Environmental Scarcities," 5–40.

230. Buhaug, Gleditsch, and Theisen, "Implications of Climate Change for Armed Conflict."

231. David P. MacKinnon et al., "A Comparison of Methods to Test Mediation and Other Intervening Variable Effects," *Psychological Methods* 7, no. 1 (March 2002): 83–104.

232. German Advisory Council on Global Change, *Security Risk*.

233. Miguel, Satyanath, and Sergenti, "Economic Shocks," 725.

234. Levy et al., "Freshwater Availability Anomalies"; Hendrix and Glaser, "Trends and Triggers," 695–715.

235. Salehyan, "From Climate Change to Conflict?," 315; Levy et al., "Freshwater Availability Anomalies"; Raleigh and Urdal, "Environmental Degradation," 674–694; Hendrix and Glaser, "Trends and Triggers," 695–715.

236. Raleigh and Urdal, "Environmental Degradation," 674–694; Theisen, "Blood and Soil?," 801; Theisen, "Other Pathways to Conflict?."

237. Amartya Sen, *Development as Freedom* (Oxford, UK: Oxford University Press, 1999).

238. Miguel, Satyanath, and Sergenti, "Economic Shocks and Civil Conflict," 725.

239. Paul Collier, Anke Hoeffler, and Dominic Rohner, "Beyond Greed and Grievance: Feasibility and Civil War," *Oxford Economic Papers* 61, no. 1 (2009): 1–27; James D. Fearon and David Laitin, "Ethnicity, Insurgency, and Civil War," *American Political Science Review* 97, no. 1 (2003): 75–90.

240. Syed Mansoob Murshed and Mohammad Zulfan Tadjoeddin, "Revisiting the Greed and Grievance Explanations for Violent Internal Conflict," *Journal of International Development* 21, no. 1 (2009): 87–111.

241. Paul Collier, "Economic Causes of Civil Conflict and their Implications for Policy," in *Leashing the Dogs of War: Conflict Management in a Divided World*, ed. Chester A. Crocker, Fen Osler Hampson, and Pamela Aall (Washington, DC: U.S. Institute of Peace Press Books, 2007); Scott Gates, "Recruitment and Allegiance: The Microfoundations of Rebellion," *The Journal of Conflict Resolution* 46, no. 1 (February 2002): 111.

242. Barnett and Adger, "Climate Change, Human Security and Violent Conflict," 639–655.

243. Teklu, Von Braun, and Zaki, *Drought and Famine*.

244. Flint and de Waal, *Darfur: A New History of a Long War*.

245. Murshed, "The Conflict-Growth Nexus."

246. Hendrix and Glaser, "Trends and Triggers," 695–715.

247. Thomas Reardon, Peter Matlon, and Christopher Delgado, "Coping with Household-Level Food Insecurity in Drought-Affected Areas of Burkina Faso," *World Development* 16, no. 9 (1988), 1065–1074; Thomas Reardon, "Using Evidence of Household Income Diversification to Inform Study of the Rural Nonfarm Labor Market in Africa," *World Development* 25, no. 8 (1997), 735–747.

248. Holsti, *The State, War, and the State of War*.

249. Patrick Meier, Doug Bond, and Joe Bond, "Environmental Influences on Pastoral Conflict in the Horn of Africa," *Political Geography* 26, no. 6 (2007): 716–735.

250. Volker Boege et al., "On Hybrid Political Orders and Emerging States: State Formation in the Context of 'Fragility,'" Berghof Research Center for Constructive Conflict Management, Berlin, 2008.

251. Anthony Nyong, "Climate-Related Conflicts in West Africa," Woodrow Wilson International Center for Scholars, *Environmental Change and Security Program Report* 12 (2006–2007): 36–43.

252. Reardon, Matlon, and Delgado, "Coping with Household-Level Food Insecurity," 1065–1074; Thomas Reardon and J. Edward Taylor, "Agroclimatic Shock, Income Inequality, and Poverty: Evidence from Burkina Faso," *World Development* 24, no. 5 (1996): 901–914.

253. Flint and de Waal, *Darfur: A New History of a Long War*.

254. Eltigani, *War and Drought in Sudan.*

255. Alex de Waal, "Famine Mortality," 5–24; Flint and de Waal, *Darfur: A New History of a Long War.*

256. Teklu, Von Braun, and Zaki, *Drought and Famine.*

257. David Carment, "Assessing State Failure: Implications for Theory and Policy," *Third World Quarterly* 24, no. 3 (2003): 407–427.

258. Nicholas Sambanis, "Do Ethnic and Nonethnic Civil Wars have the Same Causes? A Theoretical and Empirical Inquiry," *Journal of Conflict Resolution* 45, no. 3 (June 2001): 259–282; Holsti, *The State, War, and the State of War.*

259. Stergios Skaperdas, "An Economic Approach to Analyzing Civil Wars," *Economics of Governance* 9, no. 1 (2008): 25–44.

260. Colin H. Kahl, *States, Scarcity, and Civil Strife in the Developing World* (Princeton, NJ: Princeton University Press, 2006).

261. Sarah Kenyon Lischer, "Causes of Communal War: Fear and Feasibility," *Studies in Conflict & Terrorism* 22, no. 4 (1999): 331–355; Barry R. Posen, "The Security Dilemma and Ethnic Conflict," *Survival* 35, no. 1 (Spring 1993): 27–47.

262. Richard Jackson, "The Social Construction of Internal War," in *(Re)Constructing Cultures of Violence and Peace*, ed. Richard Jackson (Amsterdam and New York, NY: Rodopi, 2004), 61.

263. Flint and de Waal, *Darfur: A New History of a Long War.*

264. Jackson, "The Social Construction of Internal War," 61; Diamond, *Collapse*; Catherine André and Jean-Philippe Platteau, "Land Relations Under Unbearable Stress: Rwanda Caught in the Malthusian Trap," *Journal of Economic Behavior and Organization* 34, no. 1 (1998): 1–47; Tom Maliti, "Rwandan Panel Says Army Shot Down President's Jet," *Associated Press Worldstream* (January 12, 2010).

265. André and Platteau, "Land Relations," 1–47.

266. Carment, "Assessing State Failure," 407–427.

267. Lischer, "Causes of Communal War," 331–355.

268. Carment, "Assessing State Failure," 407–427.

269. Jonathan Goodhand and David Hulme, "From Wars to Complex Political Emergencies: Understanding Conflict and Peace-Building in the New World Disorder," *Third World Quarterly* 20, no. 1 (February 1999): 13–26; Antonio Giustozzi, "The Debate on Warlordism: The Importance of Military Legitimacy," *Crisis States Discussion Papers*, no. 13 (2005).

270. Rafael Reuveny, "Climate Change-Induced Migration and Violent Conflict," *Political Geography* 26 (2007): 656–673; Rafael Reuveny, "Ecomigration and Violent Conflict: Case Studies and Public Policy Implications," *Human Ecology*, no. 36 (2008): 1–13.

271. James N. Gregory, *American Exodus: The Dust Bowl Migration and Okie Culture in California* (New York: Oxford University Press, 1989); Donald Worster, *Dust Bowl: The Southern Plains in the 1930s* (New York: Oxford University Press, 1979).

272. Reuveny, "Climate Change-Induced Migration," 656–673.

273. Shin-wha Lee, *Environment Matters: Conflicts, Refugees & International Relations* (Seoul and Tokyo: World Human Development Institute Press, 2001); Mizanur Rahman Shelley, ed., *The Chittagong Hill Tracts of Bangladesh: The Untold Story* (Dhaka, Bangladesh: Centre for Development Research, 1992).

274. Flint and de Waal, *Darfur: A New History of a Long War*; Nielsen, "Ethnic Boundaries," 427–462.

275. Flint and de Waal, *Darfur: A New History of a Long War*; United Nations Environment Programme, *Sudan Post-Conflict Environmental Assessment*; Elke Grawert, "Cross-Border Dynamics of Violent Conflict: The Case of Sudan and Chad," *Journal of Asian and African Studies* 43, no. 6 (2008): 595–614.

276. Reuveny, "Ecomigration and Violent Conflict," 1–13.

277. Jack A. Goldstone, "Demography, Environment, and Security," in *Environmental Conflict*, ed. Paul F. Diehl and Nils Petter Gleditsch (Boulder, CO: Westview Press, 2001), 84–108; Michael S. Teitelbaum and Jay Winter, *A Question of Numbers: High Migration, Low Fertility and the Politics of National Identity* (New York: Hill and Wang, 1998).

278. Holsti, *The State, War, and the State of War*; James D. Fearon and David D. Laitin, "Review: Violence and the Social Construction of Ethnic Identity," *International Organization* 54, no. 4 (Autumn 2000): 845–877.

279. Dasgupta et al., "The Impact of Sea Level Rise on Developing Countries," 379; CNA Corporation, *National Security*; German Advisory Council on Global Change, *Security Risk*.

280. CNA Corporation, *National Security*; German Advisory Council on Global Change, *Security Risk*; Campbell, *Climatic Cataclysm*; Clionadh Raleigh, Lisa Jordan, and Idean Salehyan, "Assessing the Impact of Climate Change on Migration and Conflict" (The World Bank, "Social Dimensions of Climate Change" workshop, Washington, DC, March 5–6, 2008).

281. Tor A. Benjaminsen, "Does Supply-Induced Scarcity Drive Violent Conflicts in the African Sahel? The Case of the Tuareg Rebellion in Northern Mali," *Journal of Peace Research* 45, no. 6 (2008): 819–836; Miguel, Satyanath, and Sergenti, "Economic Shocks and Civil Conflict," 725.

282. Goldstone, "Demography, Environment, and Security," 84–108.

283. Raleigh, Jordan, and Salehyan, "Assessing the Impact of Climate Change"; Vikram Odedra Kolmannskog, *Future Floods of Refugees: A Comment on Climate Change, Conflict and Forced Migration* (Oslo: Norwegian Refugee Council, 2008); Dabelko, "Avoid Hyperbole."

284. Barnett and Adger, "Climate Change, Human Security and Violent Conflict," 639–655.

285. Ibid.; Nils Gilman, Doug Randall, and Peter Schwartz, "Impacts of Climate Change: A System Vulnerability Approach to Consider the Potential Impacts to 2050 of a Mid-Upper Greenhouse Gas Emissions Scenario," January 2007, http://media.washingtonpost.com/wp-srv/opinions/documents/gbn_impacts_of_climate_change.pdf.

286. Levy et al., "Freshwater Availability Anomalies"; Miguel, Satyanath, and Sergenti, "Economic Shocks and Civil Conflict," 725; Hendrix and Glaser, "Trends and Triggers," 695–715.

287. Ben Mohamed, Duivenbooden, and Abdoussallam, "Impact of Climate Change on Agricultural Production in the Sahel," 327–348; Teklu, Von Braun, and Zaki, *Drought and Famine*.

288. Barnett and Adger, "Climate Change, Human Security and Violent Conflict," 639–655.

289. Blake Hounshell, "2009 Failed States Index—FAQ and Methodology," Special Report, June 22, 2009, *Foreign Policy*, http://www.foreignpolicy.com/articles/2009/06/22/2009_failed_states_index_faq_methodology.

290. Barnett and Adger, "Climate Change, Human Security and Violent Conflict," 639–655; Salehyan, "From Climate Change to Conflict?," 315.

291. Dasgupta et al., "The Impact of Sea Level Rise on Developing Countries," 379; Central Intelligence Agency, "The World Factbook," accessed March 2010, https://www.cia.gov/library/publications/the-world-factbook/; Nicholls et al., "Coastal Systems and Low-Lying Areas," 315–356.

292. United Nations Development Programme, United Nations Economic and Social Council, Statistical Commission, Forty-second session, "Report of the United Nations Development Programme on Statistics of Human Development," accessed March 2012, http://unstats.un.org/unsd/statcom/doc11/2011-15-UNDP-HumanDevelopment-E.pdf (December 7, 2010).

293. The World Bank, "World Bank Journals: World Bank Economic Review and World Bank Research Observer," accessed April 2010, http://go.worldbank.org/UABDUDFPM0.

294. Hounshell, "2010 Failed States Index."

295. Dasgupta et al., "The Impact of Sea Level Rise on Developing Countries," 379.

Chapter Five

296. Chalmers, "Spending to Save?"

297. Alice Ackermann, "The Idea and Practice of Conflict Prevention," *Journal of Peace Research* 40, no. 3 (May 2003): 339–347.

298. Ibid.

299. Ibid.

300. Ibid.; Makhamadzhan Khamidov, "Mediators Provide 'First Aid' when Local Conflicts Erupt in Southern Kyrgyzstan," Organization for Security and Cooperation in Europe, December 22, 2009, accessed February 17, 2010, http://www.osce.org/bishkek/57772.

301. Jack A. Goldstone et al., "State Failure Task Force Report: Phase III Findings" (McLean, VA: State Failure Task Force, Science Applications International Corporation, 2000).

302. Grawert, "Cross-Border Dynamics of Violent Conflict," 595–614; Goldstone, "Demography, Environment, and Security," 84–108.

303. National Security Council, *National Security Strategy* (2010); National Security Council, *National Security Strategy* (2006); National Security Council, *National Security Strategy* (2002).

304. Monika François and Inder Sud, "Promoting Stability and Development in Fragile and Failed States," *Development Policy Review* 24, no. 2 (2006): 141–160.

305. Chalmers, "Spending to Save?"

306. Ibid.

307. Alan Macdonald, "Groundwater, Poverty Reduction and Climate Change," presentation at the Overseas Development Institute, London, March 22, 2010, http://www.odi.org.uk/sites/odi.org.uk/files/odi-assets/events-presentations/686.pdf; Richard Taylor, "Rethinking Water Scarcity: Role of Storage," presentation at the Overseas Development Institute, London, March 22, 2010, http://www.odi.org.uk/sites/odi.org.uk/files/odi-assets/events-presentations/687.pdf.

308. Ibid.

309. Carter et al., "New Assessment Methods," 133–171.

310. Brian Blankespoor et al., "The Economics of Adaptation to Extreme Weather Events in Developing Countries," Center for Global Development, Working Paper 199 (January 2010).

311. Carter et al., "New Assessment Methods," 133–171.

312. Gerald C. Nelson et al., "Climate Change: Impact on Agriculture and Costs of Adaptation" (Washington, DC: International Food Policy Research Institute, 2009).

313. Blankespoor et al., "The Economics of Adaptation to Extreme Weather Events."

314. Organisation for Economic Co-operation and Development, "Integrating

Climate Change Adaptation into Development Co-operation: Policy Guidance" (Paris: Organisation for Economic Co-operation and Development, 2009).

315. Ackermann, "Idea and Practice of Conflict Prevention," 339–347.

316. Robert B. Zoellick, "Fragile States: Securing Development," *Survival* 50, no. 6 (2009): 67–84.

317. Craig Burnside and David Dollar, "Aid Spurs Growth in a Sound Policy Environment," *Finance & Development* 34, no. 4 (1997): 4–7; Craig Burnside and David Dollar, "Aid, Policies, and Growth: Revisiting the Evidence," World Bank Policy Research Working Paper 3251, March 2004.

318. Mark McGillivray, "Aid Allocation and Fragile States," Discussion Paper No. 2006/01, United Nations University, World Institute for Development Economics Research, January 2006.

319. Millennium Challenge Corporation, "About MCC," http://www.mcc.gov/pages/about.

320. McGillivray, "Aid Allocation and Fragile States."

321. Victoria Levin and David Dollar, "The Forgotten States: Aid Volumes and Volatility in Difficult Partnership Countries (1992–2002)," summary paper prepared for the DAC Learning and Advisory Process on Difficult Partnership Countries Senior Level Forum, London, January 13–14, 2005.

322. Stewart Patrick and Kaysie Brown, "Fragile States and U.S. Foreign Assistance: Show Me the Money," Center for Global Development, Working Paper 26 (August 2006).

323. Nancy Birdsall, "Do No Harm: Aid, Weak Institutions and the Missing Middle in Africa," *Development Policy Review* 25, no. 5 (2007): 575–598.

324. Ibid.

325. François and Sud, "Promoting Stability and Development," 141–160.

326. Ibid.; Patrick and Brown, "Fragile States."

327. Birdsall, "Do No Harm," 575–598.

328. François and Sud, "Promoting Stability and Development," 141–160.

329. Millennium Challenge Corporation, "About MCC."

330. Boege et al., "On Hybrid Political Orders."

331. Tobias Debiel and Daniel Lambach, "How State-Building Strategies Miss Local Realities," *Peace Review* 21, no. 1 (2009): 22–28.

332. Boege et al., "On Hybrid Political Orders."

333. Meier, Bond, and Bond, "Environmental Influence on Pastoral Conflict," 716–735.

334. Boege et al., "On Hybrid Political Orders."

335. Goldstone et al., "State Failure Task Force Report: Phase III Findings"; Daniel C. Esty et al., "Working Papers: State Failure Task Force Report" (McLean, VA: State Failure Task Force, Science Applications International Corporation, 1995).

336. Reardon, Matlon, and Delgado, "Coping with Household-Level Food Insecurity," 1065–1074.

337. Alley et al., "Summary for Policymakers"; German Advisory Council on Global Change, *Security Risk*.

338. The World Bank, *World Development Report 2008: Agriculture for Development.*

339. Philip Nel and Marjolein Righarts, "Natural Disasters and the Risk of Violent Civil Conflict," *International Studies Quarterly* 52, no. 1 (2008): 159–185.

340. Gilman, Randall, and Schwartz, "Impacts of Climate Change."

Bibliography

Abdalla, Abdalla Ahmed. "Environmental Degradation and Conflict in Darfur: Experiences and Development Options." In Conference Proceedings, *Environmental Degradation as a Cause of Conflict in Darfur*. Addis Ababa, Ethiopia: University for Peace, Africa Programme, 2006.

Ackermann, Alice. "The Idea and Practice of Conflict Prevention." *Journal of Peace Research* 40, no. 3 (May 2003): 339–347.

Alley, Richard B., et al. "IPCC 2007: Summary for Policymakers." In *Contribution of Working Group I to the Fourth Assessment Report of the Intergovernmental Panel on Climate Change*. Edited by Susan Solomon et al. Cambridge, UK, and New York, NY: Cambridge University Press, 2007.

American Association for the Advancement of Science et al. "Statement on Climate Change from 18 Scientific Associations." Letter to Congress, October 21, 2009. http://www.ucsusa.org/ssi/climate-change/scientific-consensus-on.html.

André, Catherine, and Jean-Philippe Platteau. "Land Relations Under Unbearable Stress: Rwanda Caught in the Malthusian Trap." *Journal of Economic Behavior and Organization* 34, no. 1 (1998): 1–47.

Ban Ki Moon. "A Climate Culprit in Darfur." Opinion, *Washington Post*, June 16, 2007.

Barnett, Jon, and W. Neil Adger. "Climate Change, Human Security and Violent Conflict." *Political Geography* 26 (2007): 639–655.

Barth, Fredrik. *Human Resources: Social and Cultural Features of the Jebel Marra Project Area; Bergen Studies in Social Anthropology*. Bergen, Norway: Department of Social Anthropology, University of Bergen, 1988.

Bashar, Z. M. "Mechanisms for Peaceful Co-Existence among Tribal Groups in Darfur." Master's thesis, University of Khartoum, 2003.

Bassil, Noah R. "The Rise and Demise of the Keira Sultanate of Dar Fur." *Journal of North African Studies* 11, no. 4 (2006): 347–364.

Bates, Bryson, et al., eds. *Climate Change and Water*. Geneva: IPCC Secretariat, 2008.

Ben Mohamed, Abdelkrim, Niek van Duivenbooden, and Saidou Abdoussallam. "Impact of Climate Change on Agricultural Production in the Sahel—Part 1. Methodological Approach and Case Study for Millet in Niger." *Climatic Change* 54, no. 3 (August 1, 2002): 327–348.

Benjaminsen, Tor A. "Does Supply-Induced Scarcity Drive Violent Conflicts in the African Sahel? The Case of the Tuareg Rebellion in Northern Mali." *Journal of Peace Research* 45, no. 6 (2008): 819–836.

Binningsbø, Helga Malmin, Indra de Soysa, and Nils Petter Gleditsch. "Green Giant or Straw Man? Environmental Pressure and Civil Conflict, 1961–99." *Population and Environment* 28, no. 6 (2007): 337–353.

Birdsall, Nancy. "Do No Harm: Aid, Weak Institutions and the Missing Middle in Africa." *Development Policy Review* 25, no. 5 (2007): 575–598.

Blankespoor, Brian, et al. "The Economics of Adaptation to Extreme Weather Events in Developing Countries." Center for Global Development, Working Paper 199, January 2010.

Boege, Volker, et al. "On Hybrid Political Orders and Emerging States: State Formation in the Context of 'Fragility.'" Berghof Research Center for Constructive Conflict Management, Berlin, 2008.

Boko, Michel, et al. "Africa: Impacts, Adaptation and Vulnerability." In *Climate Change 2007: Impacts, Adaptation and Vulnerability; Contribution of Working Group II to the Fourth Assessment Report of the Intergovernmental Panel on Climate Change.* Cambridge, UK: Cambridge University Press, 2007, 433–467.

Bonds, Matthew H., et al. "Poverty Trap Formed by the Ecology of Infectious Diseases." *Proceedings of the Royal Society B.* December 9, 2009. http://dx.doi.org/10.1098/rspb.2009.1778.

Brown, Oli, Anne Hammill, and Robert McLeman. "Climate Change as the 'New' Security Threat: Implications for Africa." *International Affairs* 83, no. 6 (2007): 1141–1154.

Buhaug, Halvard, Nils Petter Gleditsch, and Ole Magnus Theisen. "Implications of Climate Change for Armed Conflict." The World Bank, "Social Dimensions of Climate Change" workshop, Washington, DC, March 5–6, 2008.

Buhaug, Halvard, and Päivi Lujala. "Accounting for Scale: Measuring Geography in Quantitative Studies of Civil War." *Political Geography* 24, no. 4 (2005): 399–418.

Burnside, Craig, and David Dollar. "Aid Spurs Growth in a Sound Policy Environment." *Finance & Development* 34, no. 4 (1997): 4–7.

———."Aid, Policies, and Growth: Revisiting the Evidence." World Bank Policy Research Working Paper 3251, March 2004.

Burr, J. Millard, and Robert O. Collins. *Africa's Thirty Years' War: Libya, Chad and the Sudan, 1963–1993*. Boulder, CO: Westview Press, 1999.

Campbell, Kurt, ed. *Climatic Cataclysm: The Foreign Policy and National Security Implications of Climate Change*. Washington DC: Brookings Institution Press, 2008.

Carment, David. "Assessing State Failure: Implications for Theory and Policy." *Third World Quarterly* 24, no. 3 (2003): 407–427.

Carter, Timothy R., et al. "New Assessment Methods and the Characterisation of Future Conditions." In *Climate Change 2007: Impacts, Adaptation and Vulnerability; Contribution of Working Group II to the Fourth Assessment Report of the Intergovernmental Panel on Climate Change*. Edited by Martin Parry et al. Cambridge, UK: Cambridge University Press, 2007, 133–171.

Central Intelligence Agency. "The World Factbook." Accessed March 2010. https://www.cia.gov/library/publications/the-world-factbook/.

Chalmers, Malcolm. "Spending to Save? An Analysis of the Cost Effectiveness of Conflict Prevention versus Intervention After the Onset of Violent Conflict: Phase 2 Synthesis Report." Working Papers. Bradford, UK: Bradford University, 2005.

Christensen, Jens Hesselbjerg, et al. "IPCC 2007: Regional Climate Projections." In *Contribution of Working Group I to the Fourth Assessment Report of the Intergovernmental Panel on Climate Change*. Edited by Susan Solomon et al. Cambridge, UK, and New York, NY: Cambridge University Press, 2007.

CNA Corporation. *National Security and the Threat of Climate Change*. Alexandria, VA: The CNA Corporation, 2007.

Collier, Paul, Anke Hoeffler, and Dominic Rohner. "Beyond Greed and Grievance: Feasibility and Civil War." *Oxford Economic Papers* 61, no. 1 (2009): 1–27.

Collier, Paul. "Economic Causes of Civil Conflict and their Implications for Policy." *In Leashing the Dogs of War: Conflict Management in a Divided World*. Edited by Chester A. Crocker, Fen Osler Hampson, and Pamela Aall. Washington, DC: U.S. Institute of Peace Press Books, 2007.

Collins, Robert O. *A History of Modern Sudan*. Cambridge, UK, and New York, NY: Cambridge University Press, 2008.

Commission on Macroeconomics and Health. *Macroeconomics and Health: Investing in Health for Economic Development*. Geneva, Switzerland: World Health Organization, 2001.

Confalonieri, Ulisses, et al. "Human Health." In *Climate Change 2007: Impacts, Adaptation and Vulnerability; Contribution of Working Group II to the Fourth Assessment Report of the Intergovernmental Panel on Climate Change*. Edited by Martin Parry et al. Cambridge, UK: Cambridge University Press, 2007, 391–431.

Dabelko, Geoffrey D. "Avoid Hyperbole, Oversimplification when Climate and Security Meet." In *Bulletin of the Atomic Scientists* 15, no. 7 (August 24, 2009). http://thebulletin.org/avoid-hyperbole-oversimplification-when-climate-and-security-meet.

Daly, Martin W. *Darfur's Sorrow: The Forgotten History of a Humanitarian Disaster*. Cambridge, UK, and New York, NY: Cambridge University Press, 2010.

Dasgupta, Susmita, et al. "The Impact of Sea Level Rise on Developing Countries: A Comparative Analysis." Washington, DC: The World Bank, 2007.

Davis, Mike. *Late Victorian Holocausts: El Niño Famines and the Making of the Third World*. London: Verso Books, 2001.

De Waal, Alex. "Famine Mortality: A Case Study of Darfur, Sudan 1984–5." *Population Studies* 43, no. 1 (1989): 5–24.

———. "Who are the Darfurians? Arab and African Identities, Violence and External Engagement." *African Affairs* 104, no. 415 (2005): 181.

———. "Darfur: The Inside Story." *New African* 461 (April 2007): 28–33.

———. "Is Climate Change the Culprit for Darfur?" *African Arguments* (blog), June 25, 2007. Accessed February 2010. http://africanarguments.org/2007/06/25/is-climate-change-the-culprit-for-darfur/.

Debiel, Tobias, and Daniel Lambach. "How State-Building Strategies Miss Local Realities." *Peace Review* 21, no. 1 (2009): 22–28.

Degomme, Olivier, and Debarati Guha-Sapir. "Patterns of Mortality Rates in Darfur Conflict." *The Lancet* 375, no. 9711 (2010): 294–300.

Diamond, Jared. *Collapse: How Societies Choose to Fail Or Succeed.* New York: Penguin Books, 2006.

DiMento, Joseph F. C., and Pamela Doughman, eds. *Climate Change: What It Means for Us, Our Children, and Our Grandchildren.* Cambridge, MA: MIT Press, 2007.

Doornbos, Paul. "On Becoming Sudanese: Aspects of Ideological Transformation in Rural Sudan." Paper presented at the Workshop on Capital, State, and Transformation in Sudan. Edited by Tony Barnett and Abbas Abdelkarim. London: Croom Helm, 1988: 99–121.

Edwards, Scott. "Social Breakdown in Darfur." *Forced Migration Review* 31 (October 2008): 23.

Eltigani, Eltigani E., ed. *War and Drought in Sudan: Essays on Population Displacement.* Gainesville, FL: University Press of Florida, 1995.

Esty, Daniel C., et al. "Working Papers: State Failure Task Force Report." McLean, VA: State Failure Task Force, Science Applications International Corporation, 1995.

Faris, Stephan. "The Real Roots of Darfur." *Atlantic*, April 2007.

Fearon, James D., and David Laitin. "Review: Violence and the Social Construction of Ethnic Identity." *International Organization* 54, no. 4 (Autumn 2000): 845–877.

———. "Ethnicity, Insurgency, and Civil War." *American Political Science Review* 97, no. 1 (2003): 75–90.

Flint, Julie, and Alex de Waal. *Darfur: A New History of a Long War.* London and New York, NY: Zed Books Ltd, 2008.

————. "Case Closed: A Prosecutor without Borders." *World Affairs* 171, no. 4 (Spring 2009): 23–38.

François, Monika, and Inder Sud. "Promoting Stability and Development in Fragile and Failed States." *Development Policy Review* 24, no. 2 (2006): 141–160.

Gates, Scott. "Recruitment and Allegiance: The Microfoundations of Rebellion." *The Journal of Conflict Resolution* 46, no. 1 (February 2002): 111.

Gebresenbet, Fana. "Climate and Vegetation Changes in the Sahel: The Case of Darfur." In *Environment and Conflict in Africa: Reflections on Darfur.* Edited by Marcel Leroy. Addis Ababa, Ethiopia: University for Peace, Africa Programme, 2009, 14–26.

Gerlak, Andrea K., and Keith A. Grant. "The Correlates of Cooperative Institutions for International Rivers." In *Mapping the New World Order.* Edited by Thomas J. Volgy et al. Malden, MA: Wiley-Blackwell, 2009, 114–147.

German Advisory Council on Global Change. *Climate Change as a Security Risk.* London and Sterling, VA: Earthscan, 2008.

Giannini, Alessandra, Michela Biasutti, and Michel M. Verstraete. "A Climate Model-Based Review of Drought in the Sahel: Desertification, the Re-Greening and Climate Change." *Global and Planetary Change* 64, no. 3–4 (December 2008): 119–128.

Gilman, Nils, Doug Randall, and Peter Schwartz. "Impacts of Climate Change: A System Vulnerability Approach to Consider the Potential Impacts to 2050 of a Mid-Upper Greenhouse Gas Emissions Scenario." January 2007. http://media.washingtonpost.com/wp-srv/opinions/documents/gbn_impacts_of_climate_change.pdf.

Giustozzi, Antonio. "The Debate on Warlordism: The Importance of Military Legitimacy." *Crisis States Discussion Papers*, no. 13 (2005).

Gleditsch, Nils Petter, et al. "Armed Conflict 1946–2001: A New Dataset." *Journal of Peace Research* 39, no. 5 (2002), 615–637.

————. "Conflicts Over Shared Rivers: Resource Scarcity Or Fuzzy Boundaries?" *Political Geography* 25 (2006), 361–382.

Gleick, Peter H. "Water and Conflict: Fresh Water Resources and International Security." *International Security* 18, no. 1 (Summer 1993): 79–112.

Gleick, Peter H., Ashbindu Singh, and Hua Shi. *Emerging Threats to the World's Freshwater Resources.* Oakland, CA: Pacific Institute for Studies in Development, Environment, and Security, 2002.

Goldstone, Jack A. "Demography, Environment, and Security." In *Environmental Conflict.* Edited by Paul F. Diehl and Nils Petter Gleditsch. Boulder, CO: Westview Press, 2001, 84–108.

Goldstone, Jack A., et al. "State Failure Task Force Report: Phase III Findings." McLean, VA: State Failure Task Force, Science Applications International Corporation, 2000.

Goodhand, Jonathan, and David Hulme. "From Wars to Complex Political Emergencies: Understanding Conflict and Peace-Building in the New World Disorder." *Third World Quarterly* 20, no. 1 (February 1999): 13–26.

Grawert, Elke. "Cross-Border Dynamics of Violent Conflict: The Case of Sudan and Chad." *Journal of Asian and African Studies* 43, no. 6 (2008): 595–614.

Gregory, James N. *American Exodus: The Dust Bowl Migration and Okie Culture in California.* New York: Oxford University Press, 1989.

Hagan, John, and Wenona Rymond-Richmond. *Darfur and the Crime of Genocide.* Cambridge, UK: Cambridge University Press, 2008.

Harir, Sharif. "'Arab Belt' Versus 'African Belt': Ethno-Political Conflict in Dar Fur and the Regional Cultural Factors." In *Shortcut to Decay: The Case of Sudan.* Edited by Sharif Harir and Terje Tvedt. Motala, Sweden: Nordiska Afrikainstitutet, 1994, 144–185.

Hauge, Wenche, and Tanja Ellingsen. "Beyond Environmental Scarcity: Causal Pathways to Conflict." *Journal of Peace Research* 35, no. 3 (1998), 299.

Hendrix, Cullen S., and Sarah M. Glaser. "Trends and Triggers: Climate, Climate Change and Civil Conflict in Sub-Saharan Africa." *Political Geography* 26 (2007), 695–715.

Holsti, Kalevi J. *The State, War, and the State of War.* Cambridge, UK: Cambridge University Press, 1996.

Homer-Dixon, Thomas F. "Environmental Scarcities and Violent Conflict: Evidence from Cases." *International Security* 19, no. 1 (1994): 5–40.

———. "Positive Feedbacks, Dynamic Ice Sheets, and the Recarbonization of the Global Fuel Supply: The New Sense of Urgency about Global Warming." In *A Globally Integrated Climate Policy for Canada.* Edited by Steven Bernstein et al. Toronto: University of Toronto Press, 2007, 37–54.

———. "Straw Man in the Wind." *The National Interest* Jan/Feb 2008, no. 93 (2008): 26.

Horton, Radley, et al. "Sea Level Rise Projections for Current Generation CGCMs Based on the Semi-Empirical Method." *Geophysical Research Letters* 35, no. L02715 (2008).

Hounshell, Blake. "2009 Failed States Index: FAQ and Methodology." Special Report, June 22, 2009. *Foreign Policy,* http://www.foreignpolicy.com/articles/2009/06/22/2009_failed_states_index_faq_methodology.

International Food Policy Research Institute (IFPRI). *Climate Change: Impact on Agriculture and Costs of Adaptation.* Edited by Gerald C. Nelson et al. Washington, DC: International Food Policy Research Institute, 2009.

International Criminal Court. "Fourth Report of the Prosecutor of the International Criminal Court, Mr. Luis Moreno Ocampo, to the UN Security Council Pursuant to UNSCR 1593 (2005)." December 14, 2006. http://www.icc-cpi.int/NR/rdonlyres/19B2F772-E5E3-4DBB-8B0F-5A220DB958F3/277803/OTP_ReportUNSC4Darfur_English.pdf.

Jackson, Richard. "The Social Construction of Internal War." In *(Re)Constructing Cultures of Violence and Peace.* Edited by Richard Jackson. Amsterdam and New York, NY: Rodopi, 2004, 61.

Kahl, Colin H. *States, Scarcity, and Civil Strife in the Developing World.* Princeton, NJ: Princeton University Press, 2006.

Kandji, Serigne Tacko, Louis Verchot, and Jens Mackensen. *Climatic Change and Variability in the Sahel Region: Impacts and Adaptation Strategies in the Agricultural Sector.* Nairobi, Kenya: United Nations Environment Programme and the World Agroforestry Centre, 2006.

Kevane, Michael, and Leslie Gray. "Darfur: Rainfall and Conflict." *Environmental Research Letters* 3 (2008): 034006.

Khamidov, Makhamadzhan. "Mediators Provide 'First Aid' when Local Conflicts Erupt in Southern Kyrgyzstan." Organization for Security and Cooperation in Europe, December 22, 2009. Accessed February 17, 2010. http://www.osce.org/bishkek/57772.

King, Mary, and Mohamed Awad Osman. "Executive Summary." In Conference Proceedings, *Environmental Degradation as a Cause of Conflict in Darfur.* Addis Ababa, Ethiopia: University for Peace, Africa Programme, 2006.

Kolmannskog, Vikram Odedra. *Future Floods of Refugees: A Comment on Climate Change, Conflict and Forced Migration.* Oslo: Norwegian Refugee Council, 2008.

Leary, Neil, and Jyoti Kulkarni. "Climate Change Vulnerability and Adaptation in Developing Country Regions." Washington, DC: The International START Secretariat, and Trieste, Italy: The Academy of Sciences for the Developing World, 2007.

Lee, Shin-wha. *Environment Matters: Conflicts, Refugees & International Relations.* Seoul and Tokyo: World Human Development Institute Press, 2001.

Leroy, Marcel, ed. *Environment and Conflict in Africa: Reflections on Darfur.* Addis Ababa, Ethiopia: University for Peace, Africa Programme, 2009.

Levin, Victoria, and David Dollar. "The Forgotten States: Aid Volumes and Volatility in Difficult Partnership Countries (1992–2002)." Summary paper prepared for the DAC Learning and Advisory Process on Difficult Partnership Countries Senior Level Forum, London, January 13–14, 2005.

Levy, Marc A., et al. "Freshwater Availability Anomalies and Outbreak of Internal War: Results from a Global Spatial Time Series Analysis." Paper presented at the Human Security and Climate Change International Workshop, Holmen Fjord Hotel, Asker, near Oslo, June 21–23, 2005.

Lischer, Sarah Kenyon. "Causes of Communal War: Fear and Feasibility." *Studies in Conflict & Terrorism* 22, no. 4 (1999): 331–355.

Macdonald, Alan. "Groundwater, Poverty Reduction and Climate Change." Presentation at the Overseas Development Institute, London, March 22, 2010. http://www.odi.org.uk/sites/odi.org.uk/files/odi-assets events-presentations/686.pdf.

MacKinnon, David P., et al. "A Comparison of Methods to Test Mediation and Other Intervening Variable Effects." *Psychological Methods* 7, no. 1 (March 2002): 83–104.

Maliti, Tom. "Rwandan Panel Says Army Shot Down President's Jet." *Associated Press Worldstream*, January 12, 2010.

Mamdani, Mahmood. "'There May have been No Water, but the Province was Awash with Guns.'" *New Statesman* 138, no. 4952 (2009): 34–37.

McGillivray, Mark. "Aid Allocation and Fragile States." Discussion Paper No. 2006/01. United Nations University, World Institute for Development Economics Research, January 2006.

Meehl, Gerald A., et al. "Global Climate Projections." In *Climate Change 2007: The Physical Science Basis; Contribution of Working Group I to the Fourth Assessment Report of the Intergovernmental Panel on Climate Change.* Edited by Susan Solomon et al. Cambridge, UK, and New York, NY: Cambridge University Press, 2007.

Meier, Patrick, Doug Bond, and Joe Bond. "Environmental Influences on Pastoral Conflict in the Horn of Africa." *Political Geography* 26, no. 6 (2007): 716–735.

Miguel, Edward, Shanker Satyanath, and Ernest Sergenti. "Economic Shocks and Civil Conflict: An Instrumental Variables Approach." *Journal of Political Economy* 112, no. 4 (2004), 725.

Millennium Challenge Corporation. "About MCC." Accessed May 13, 2010. http://www.mcc.gov/pages/about.

Mohamed, Adam Azzain. "Indigenous Institutions and Practices Promoting Peace and/or Mitigating Conflicts: The Case of Southern Darfur of Western Sudan." In Conference Proceedings, *Environmental Degradation as a Cause of Conflict in Darfur.* Addis Ababa, Ethiopia: University for Peace, Africa Programme, 2006.

Murshed, Syed Mansoob. "The Conflict-Growth Nexus and the Poverty of Nations." United Nations Department of Economics and Social Affairs Working Paper No. 43 (June 2007).

Murshed, Syed Mansoob, and Mohammad Zulfan Tadjoeddin. "Revisiting the Greed and Grievance Explanations for Violent Internal Conflict." *Journal of International Development* 21, no. 1 (2009): 87–111.

National Academies. "Joint Science Academies' Statement: Global Response to Climate Change." 2005. http://www.nationalacademies.org/onpi/06072005.pdf.

National Security Council. *The National Security Strategy of the United States of America.* Washington, DC: U.S. Government Printing Office, 2002.

———. *The National Security Strategy of the United States of America.* Washington, DC: U.S. Government Printing Office, 2006.

———. *National Security Strategy.* Washington, DC: U.S. Government Printing Office, 2010.

Nel, Philip, and Marjolein Righarts. "Natural Disasters and the Risk of Violent Civil Conflict." *International Studies Quarterly* 52, no. 1 (2008): 159–185.

Nelson, Gerald C., et al. "Climate Change: Impact on Agriculture and Costs of Adaptation." Washington, DC: International Food Policy Research Institute, 2009.

Nicholls, Robert J., et al. "Coastal Systems and Low-Lying Areas." In *Climate Change 2007: Impacts, Adaptation and Vulnerability; Contribution of Working Group II to the Fourth Assessment Report of the Intergovernmental Panel on Climate Change.* Edited by Martin Parry et al. Cambridge, UK: Cambridge University Press, 2007, 315–356.

Nielsen, Erik Solevad. "Ethnic Boundaries and Conflict in Darfur: An Event Structure Hypothesis." *Ethnicities* 8, no. 4 (December 2008): 427–462.

Nunn, Patrick D. "The A.D. 1300 Event in the Pacific Basin." *The Geographical Review* 97, no. 1 (2007), 1–23.

Nyong, Anthony Okon. "Climate-Related Conflicts in West Africa." Woodrow Wilson International Center for Scholars. *Environmental Change and Security Program Report* 12 (2006–2007): 36–43.

————. "Climate Change, Agriculture and Trade: Implications for Sustainable Development." Paper prepared for the International Centre for Trade and Sustainable Development (ICTSD) and the session titled "Agriculture, Climate Change and Sustainable Development" at The Future of Agriculture: A Global Dialogue amongst Stakeholders, Barcelona, May 30–31, 2008.

O'Brien, Karen, et al. "Mapping Vulnerability to Multiple Stressors: Climate Change and Globalization in India." *Global Environmental Change* 14, no. 4 (2004): 303–313.

O'Fahey, Rex Sean. "Conflict in Darfur: Historical and Contemporary Perspectives." In Conference Proceedings, *Environmental Degradation as a Cause of Conflict in Darfur*. Addis Ababa, Ethiopia: University for Peace, Africa Programme, 2006.

————. *The Darfur Sultanate: A History.* New York, NY: Columbia University Press, 2008.

Olsson, Lennart, and Mryka Hall-Beyer. "Greening of the Sahel." In *Encyclopedia of Earth*. Edited by Cutler J. Cleveland. Washington, DC: Environmental Information Coalition, National Council for Science and the Environment, 2008.

Oreskes, Naomi. "Beyond the Ivory Tower: The Scientific Consensus on Climate Change." *Science* 306, no. 5702 (December 2004), 1686.

Organisation for Economic Co-operation and Development. "Integrating Climate Change Adaptation into Development Co-operation: Policy Guidance." Paris: Organisation for Economic Co-operation and Development, 2009.

Organization for Security and Cooperation in Europe. Factsheet, "What is the OSCE?" April 29, 2013. http://www.osce.org/secretariat/35775.

Parry, Martin L., et al., eds. *Climate Change 2007: Impacts, Adaptation and Vulnerability; Contribution of Working Group II to the Fourth Assessment Report of the Intergovernmental Panel on Climate Change.* Cambridge, UK: Cambridge University Press, 2007.

Patrick, Stewart, and Kaysie Brown. "Fragile States and U.S. Foreign Assistance: Show Me the Money." Center for Global Development, Working Paper 26 (August 2006).

Posen, Barry R. "The Security Dilemma and Ethnic Conflict." *Survival* 35, no. 1 (Spring 1993): 27–47.

Raleigh, Clionadh, and Henrik Urdal. "Climate Change, Environmental Degradation and Armed Conflict." *Political Geography* 26 (2007), 674–694.

Raleigh, Clionadh, Lisa Jordan, and Idean Salehyan. "Assessing the Impact of Climate Change on Migration and Conflict." The World Bank, "Social Dimensions of Climate Change" workshop, Washington, DC, March 5–6, 2008.

Randall, David A., et al. "Climate Models and their Evaluation." In *Climate Change 2007: The Physical Science Basis; Contribution of Working Group I to the Fourth Assessment Report of the Intergovernmental Panel on Climate Change.* Edited by Susan Solomon et al. Cambridge, UK, and New York, NY: Cambridge University Press, 2007.

Reardon, Thomas. "Using Evidence of Household Income Diversification to Inform Study of the Rural Nonfarm Labor Market in Africa." *World Development* 25, no. 8 (1997), 735–747.

Reardon, Thomas, Peter Matlon, and Christopher Delgado. "Coping with Household-Level Food Insecurity in Drought-Affected Areas of Burkina Faso." *World Development* 16, no. 9 (1988): 1065–1074.

Reardon, Thomas, and J. Edward Taylor. "Agroclimatic Shock, Income Inequality, and Poverty: Evidence from Burkina Faso." *World Development* 24, no. 5 (1996): 901–914.

Reuveny, Rafael. "Climate Change-Induced Migration and Violent Conflict." *Political Geography* 26 (2007): 656–673.

————. "Ecomigration and Violent Conflict: Case Studies and Public Policy Implications." *Human Ecology*, no. 36 (2008): 1–13.

Robinson, Arthur E. "The Arab Dynasty of Dar for (Darfur) A. D. 1448–1874 or A. H. 852–1201: Part I." *Journal of the Royal African Society* 27, no. 108 (July 1928): 353–363.

Salehyan, Idean. "From Climate Change to Conflict? No Consensus Yet." *Journal of Peace Research* 45, no. 3 (2008): 315.

Sambanis, Nicholas. "Do Ethnic and Nonethnic Civil Wars have the Same Causes? A Theoretical and Empirical Inquiry." *Journal of Conflict Resolution* 45, no. 3 (June 2001): 259–282.

Sandole, Dennis J. D. "Virulent Ethnocentrism: A Major Challenge for Transformational Conflict Resolution and Peacebuilding in the Post–Cold War Era." *Ethnopolitics* 1, no. 4 (2002): 4–27.

Sen, Amartya. *Development as Freedom*. Oxford, UK: Oxford University Press, 1999.

Shelley, Mizanur Rahman, ed. *The Chittagong Hill Tracts of Bangladesh: The Untold Story*. Dhaka, Bangladesh: Centre for Development Research, 1992.

Skaperdas, Stergios. "An Economic Approach to Analyzing Civil Wars." *Economics of Governance* 9, no. 1 (2008): 25–44.

Smith, Dan, and Janani Vivekananda. "A Climate of Conflict: The Links between Climate Change, Peace and War." *International Alert* (London, 2007).

Solomon, Susan, et al. "IPCC 2007: The Physical Science Basis." In *Contribution of Working Group I to the Fourth Assessment Report of the Intergovernmental Panel on Climate Change*. Edited by Susan Solomon et al. Cambridge, UK, and New York, NY: Cambridge University Press, 2007.

Starr, Joyce R. "Water Wars." *Foreign Policy* 82 (Spring 1991): 17–36.

Sutherst, Robert W. "Global Change and Human Vulnerability to Vector-Borne Diseases." *Clinical Microbiology Reviews* 17, no. 1 (January 2004): 136–173.

Taylor, Richard. "Rethinking Water Scarcity: Role of Storage." Presentation at the Overseas Development Institute, London, March 22, 2010. http://www.odi.org.uk/sites/odi.org.uk/files/odi-assetsevents-presentations/687.pdf.

Teitelbaum, Michael S., and Jay Winter. *A Question of Numbers: High Migration, Low Fertility and the Politics of National Identity*. New York: Hill and Wang, 1998.

Teklu, Tesfaye, Joachim Von Braun, and Elsayed Ali Ahmed Zaki. *Drought and Famine Relationships in Sudan: Policy Implications*. Washington, DC: International Food Policy Research Institute, 1991.

Theisen, Ole Magnus. "Other Pathways to Conflict? Environmental Scarcities and Domestic Conflict." Paper presented at the 47th Annual Convention of the International Studies Association, San Diego, CA, March 22–25, 2006.

———. "Blood and Soil? Resource Scarcity and Internal Armed Conflict Revisited." *Journal of Peace Research* 45, no. 6 (2008), 801.

Tol, Richard S. J., and Sebastian Wagner. "Climate Change and Violent Conflict in Europe Over the Last Millennium." *Climatic Change* 99, no. 1–2 (2010). http://dx.doi.org/10.1007/s10584-009-9659-2.

U.S. Department of State. "Background Note: Sudan." Accessed March 17, 2010. Originally published at http://www.state.gov/r/pa/ei/bgn/5424.htm.

United Nations, Department of Economic and Social Affairs, Population Division. *World Population Prospects: The 2008 Revision*. New York, NY: United Nations, 2009.

United Nations Development Programme. "Hunger is the Lack of Rain." Newsroom. Accessed December 1, 2009. http://content.undp.org/go/newsroom/2009/november/hunger-is-the-lack-of-rain.en.

United Nations Development Programme, United Nations Economic and Social Council, Statistical Commission, Forty-second session. "Report of the United Nations Development Programme on Statistics of Human Development." Accessed March 2012. http://unstats.un.org/unsd/statcom/doc11/2011-15-UNDP-HumanDevelopment-E.pdf (December 7, 2010).

United Nations Environment Programme. *Sudan: Post-Conflict Environmental Assessment*. Nairobi, Kenya: United Nations Environment Programme, 2007.

United Nations Intergovernmental Panel on Climate Change. *Climate Change 2001: IPCC Third Assessment Report.* http://www.grida.no/publications/other/ipcc_tar/.

Wigley, Tom M. L., et al. "Implications of Proposed CO_2 Emissions Limitations." Technical Paper 4, Intergovernmental Panel on Climate Change (1997).

Wolf, Aaron T., et al. "Water Can be a Pathway to Peace, Not War." *Navigating Peace 1* (Woodrow Wilson International Center for Scholars, 2006).

World Bank. *World Development Report 2008: Agriculture for Development.* Washington, DC: The World Bank, 2007.

———. *World Development Report 2010: Development and Climate Change.* Washington, DC: The World Bank, 2010.

———. "World Bank Journals: World Bank Economic Review and World Bank Research Observer." Accessed April 2010. http://go.worldbank.org/UABDUDFPM0.

World Health Organization. *The World Health Report 2004: Changing History.* Geneva, Switzerland: World Health Organization, 2004.

Worster, Donald. *Dust Bowl: The Southern Plains in the 1930s.* New York: Oxford University Press, 1979.

Yoffe, Shira, Aaron T. Wolf, and Mark Giordano. "Conflict and Cooperation Over International Freshwater Resources: Indicators of Basins at Risk." *Journal of the American Water Resources Association* 39, no. 5 (2003): 1109–1126.

Zeitoun, Mark, and Naho Mirumachi. "Transboundary Water Interaction I: Reconsidering Conflict and Cooperation." *International Environmental Agreements: Politics, Law & Economics* 8, no. 4 (2008): 297–316.

Zhang, David D., et al. "Climatic Change, Wars and Dynastic Cycles in China Over the Last Millennium." *Climatic Change* 76 (2006), 459–477.

Zoellick, Robert B. "Fragile States: Securing Development." *Survival* 50, no. 6 (2009): 67–84.

www.ingramcontent.com/pod-product-compliance
Lightning Source LLC
Chambersburg PA
CBHW072046280526
45788CB00006B/2200